Contents

INDEX ON CENSORSHIP
VOLUME 44 NUMBER 01
SPRING 2015

T0343925

In focus

Culture

92-94 TOOLEY STREET, LONDON SE1 2TH
+44 (0) 207 260 2660
REGISTERED CHARITY (ENGLAND AND WALES) NO. 325003

EDITOR
RACHAEL JOLLEY
DEPUTY EDITOR
VICKY BAKER
SUB EDITORS
SALLY GIMSON, PAUL ANDERSON
CONTRIBUTING EDITORS:
KAYA GENÇ (TURKEY), NATASHA JOSEPH
(SOUTH AFRICA), JEMIMAH STENFIELD

EDITORIAL ASSISTANT:
Aimée Hamilton
THANKS TO: Jodie Ginsberg, Sean Gallagher,
Milana Knežević, Matthew Hasteley,
Brett Biedscheid, Will Haydon

Supported by
ARTS COUNCIL
ENGLAND

Power outage

by **Rachael Jolley**

EDITORIAL

44(1): 3/5 | DOI: 10.1177/0306422015572973

NOTHING IS NATIONAL any more, everything and everyone is connected internationally: economies, communication systems, immigration patterns, wars and conflicts all map across networks of different kinds.

Those linking networks can leave the world better informed and more aware of its connections, or those networks can fail to acknowledge their intersections, while carrying as much misinformation as information.

Where people are living in fear a connected world can be frightening, it can carry gossip and information back to those who pursue them. Decades ago, when people escaped from their homes to make a new life across the world, they were not afraid that their words, criticising the government they had fled from, could instantly be broadcast in the land they had left behind.

It is no wonder that in this more connected world, those fleeing persecution are more afraid to tell the truth about what the regime that tortured or imprisoned them has been doing. While, on the one hand, it should be easier to find out about such horrors, the way that your words can fly around the world in seconds adds enormous pressures not to speak about, or criticise, the country you fled from.

That fear often produces silence, leaving the wider world confused about the situation in a conflict-riven country where people are being killed, threatened or imprisoned. The consequences of instant communication can be terrifyingly swift.

Yet a different side of those networks, new apps or free phone services such as Skype, can provide some help in getting messages back to families left behind, giving them some hope about their loved ones' future. That is one aspect that those in decades and centuries past, who fled their homelands, could never do. In the late 19th century, someone who escaped torture in Russia and travelled thousands of miles to the United States, might never speak to the family they had left behind again.

Communication has been revolutionised in the last two decades – where once a creaky telephone line was the only way of speaking to a sister or father across a continent or two, now Skype, Viber, Googlechat, and others offer options to see and speak every day.

In this issue's special report Across the Wires, our writers and artists examine the threats of free expression within refugee camps, and as refugees desperately flee from persecution. The UN estimates that there are 15.5 million refugees in the world today. Some are forced to live in camps for decades, others are fleeing from new conflicts, such as three million who have already left Syria. Many of us may know someone who has been forced to flee from another regime, those that don't may in the future, and have some understanding of what that journey is like.

In this issue, writer Jason DaPonte examines how those who have escaped remain worried that their words will be captured and used against their families, and the →

ABOVE: Kurdish refugee children from the Syrian town of Kobani sit behind a fence in a camp on the Turkish/Syrian border

→ steps they take to try avoid this. He also looks at "new" technology's ability to keep refugees in touch with the outside world and to help tell the story of the camps themselves.

Italian journalist Fabrizio Gatti spent four years undercover, discovering details of refugee escape routes and people trafficking. In an extract from his book, previously unpublished in English, he tells his story of assuming the identity of a Kurdish man Bilal escaping torture, and fleeing to Italy via the Lampedusa detention camp, and the treatment he encountered. He speaks only Arabic and English to camp officials, but is able to hear what they said to each other in Italian about those seeking asylum. He uncovers the inhumanity and lack of rights those around him experienced in this powerful piece of writing.

Some of our authors in this issue speak from personal experience of seeking refuge, not speaking the language of the land they are forced to move to, and the steps they go through to resettle and be accepted in another land. Kao Kalia Yang's family fled Laos during the Vietnam war, moving first to Thailand and then to the United States. She remembers how the family struggled first without understanding or speaking in Thai, then the same battles with English once they settled in the United States.

Ismail Einashe, whose family fled from Somaliland, talks to those who have escaped from one of the most secretive countries in the world, Eritrea. Einashe talks to Eritreans, now living in the UK, who are still afraid to speak openly about the conditions at home for fear of retribution.

The report also examines how the global media portrays refugee stories, the accuracy of those portrayals and how projects such as a new Syrian soap opera, partly written by a refugee, are giving asylum seekers and camp dwellers more power to tell the stories themselves.

But when people are escaping danger, the natural inclination is to stay quiet and under the radar. Some bravely do not. They intend to alert the world to a situation that is unfolding, and to attempt to protect others. Our report shows how much easier it is for the world's citizens to find out about terrible persecution than it was in other eras, but how those communication tools can be turned back on those that are persecuted

That fear often produces silence, leaving the wider world confused about the situation in a conflict-riven country where people are being killed, threatened or imprisoned

themselves. The push and pull of global networks, to be used for freedom or to silence others, is an on-going battle and one that we can only become more aware of. ☒

© Rachael Jolley
www.indexoncensorship.org

Rachael Jolley is editor of Index on Censorship magazine. Follow the magazine @index_magazine

ABOVE: Sub-Saharan Africans reach out to NGO workers on a rescue boat organised by a privately funded humanitarian initiative that assists migrants crossing from Libya to Europe

SPECIAL REPORT

In this section

Undercover immigrant

44(1): 8/14 | DOI: 10.1177/0306422015571087

Italian investigative journalist **Fabrizio Gatti** spent four years secretly travelling refugee routes across the Sahara. Assuming the role of a Kurdish asylum seeker, he was caught adrift in the Mediterranean, interrogated, and detained at Lampedusa detention camp. Here we translate an extract of his book into English for the first time

ITALIAN REPORTER FABRIZIO Gatti did not enter Lampedusa's immigration reception centre as a journalist. At least not openly so. No journalists or laywers were allowed. He entered as Bilal, a Kurdish asylum seeker – an identity he had assumed first to gain an inside perspective on how undocumented immigrants are treated on arrival in Europe. His story – written in the third-person – was published in Italian as Bilal: Travelling, Working and Dying Illegally in 2008, three years after he entered the camp.

Lampedusa, a tiny Italian island between Africa and Europe, made worldwide headlines in October 2013 when a boat sunk off its coast, killing over 360 passengers, mostly Eritreans attempting to flee the military dictatorship and forced conscription.

Ten years since Gatti took that trip, immigrants continue to make the same journey. Naval boats now patrol the waters, attempting to avert another tragedy – but not without criticism, from those saying this is not sufficient protection to others saying it encourages more to take the trip.

As Bilal, Gatti was aware of the rights he should be given. After four years spent travelling migrant routes from Africa, he simultaneously fitted in and pushed boundaries to test support mechanisms, often finding them inhumanely lacking. Although

he was able to understand Italian authorities as they interrogated him, he pretended he didn't. The book, part of which is published below, has been translated into French, German, Norwegian and Swedish, but, as yet, is not available in English. This abridged extract recounts Gatti/Bilal's treatment after being picked up from the sea and transferred to Lampedusa.

"He's hypothermic," says the doctor to a nurse, in Italian, after checking Bilal's hands and feet. "Get a bottle of saline solution and put it in some hot water. When it's warm, we'll inject it. He can't have been in the sea for long. But the water temperature's dropped to 19 degrees."

Lampedusa has been an international crossroad for years. Yet no one has taught these aid workers to speak English. Or even French. Let alone Arabic. A nurse gestures that Bilal should strip off his sodden clothes. Off come the black trousers. The cotton T-shirt. The blue sweatshirt. The heavy fleece that had glistened with plankton.

"Everything. No, no!" shouts the nurse. "Not boxers."

Bilal lies back on the bed. They insert a needle for the drip, attach the electrodes for an electrocardiogram. A different nurse with a sweet face comes closer. She looks at him. "Have you pain?" she asks, in a whisper, in English.

"Pain?"

"Yes, have you pain?" she repeats, ending the question with a smile.

"No pain. No pain."

Instead Bilal wants to know if the *carabinieri* [Italian military police] have been informed, if he will be put in the large cage. He asks a few questions. But the nurse doesn't know how to say anything else in English.

"Heart rate normal," states the doctor, removing the electrodes. The nurses measure his blood pressure. Normal. The nurse with the sweet face comes back with a glass of hot milk. [...]

Another nurse finishes writing the medical report. "What did the *carabinieri* say? Are they coming?" she asks her colleagues.

"*Adesso tu vai con i carabinieri* [Now, off you go with the carabinieri]," says another nurse, addressing Bilal.

Bilal listens. The other nurse realises he hasn't understood. "You, carabinieri, police," she translates into English.

"Police, no police," Bilal pleads and looks at the young nurse.

"*Eh, tesoro mio, che ci devo fare*? [Sorry, love, there's not much I can do, is there?] We have to hand you over to the *carabinieri*." Bilal is at the end of the line. Even she doesn't make the effort to speak English any more.

The carabinieri arrive. The women leave. Bilal is asked to take off his boxers too. "They're wet," says a male nurse. "Put on these dry clothes."

He's handed a blue outfit, the type worn in an operating theatre. But it must have been washed in boiling water. The trousers have shrunk and they barely cover his groin. The top is so tight that Bilal finds it impossible to lift his arms. The male nurse struggles to smother a laugh. "Sorry, mate," he says, "but we don't have anything else."

Bilal smiles to thank him.

The carabinieri walk quickly. Too quickly for their stiff trousers. They lock Bilal into their black car. The headlamps rake across the deserted town. They stop in a dead-end road beside the airport. On the right, at the end, is a green gate topped with a bundle of barbed wire. One officer opens it. He's dressed in riot gear, complete with heavy-duty boots and a pistol in its holster.

The noble sentiments of humanity end here, on this side of the gate. That common sentiment that binds us together as individuals, individuals who are free to think. That sentiment that draws no distinction between men and women. That forgets who they are. Friends or enemies. Fellow countrymen or foreigners. Citizens or illegal migrants.

By law, the people held inside are free citizens. So free that they're not allowed out again

Here ends that magnificent sentiment that prompted an unknown inhabitant of Lampedusa to lend me his shirt last night and warm my shivering body with his own. The same sentiment that filled the emergency nurse with smiles. Beyond this gate, state conventions come into play. Their governments' lies. The betrayal of their parliaments. Thanks to this green gate we are no longer individuals. We are what we are.

Bilal walks awkwardly between the carabinieri.

"A&E have sent us this one," say the two military police to their colleague in riot gear. By law, the Italian constitution, the European Convention on Human Rights, the Universal Declaration of Human Rights, the people held inside here are free citizens. So free that they're not allowed out again. Bilal is →

→ accompanied, head hanging, to a small courtyard where other carabinieri are waiting with a young man dressed in the yellow uniform of the private firm that runs the centre. The youngster offers Bilal a glass of water and four packs of croissants. Then he pulls a cotton T-shirt and a tracksuit out of a bag. It's a white tracksuit with four blue stripes on the sides. "Put this on. You'll be warmer," he says.

Choosing the language of interregation is top of the list of "migrants' rights", typed up and pinned up in the corridor

"What's your name? Where are you from?" asks one of the carabinieri in Italian.

"I don't understand," whispers Bilal.

The question comes again, this time in broken English. "What is ze contry you are from?"

"Kurdistan."

"Kurdistan? But this guy's whiter than me! How can he be Kurdish?" replies the carabiniere in Sicilian.

Another heavily tanned carabiniere jokes, in rhyme: "*Io sì che sono nivuro e potrei essere curdo*." (Look at me, I'm so black I could be a Kurd.)

Bilal keeps his eyes down, looking at his worn slippers, and listens to the men's banter in Italian.

"A Kurd who speaks English. Well, what d'you know? You don't think he could be an American journalist from CNN who's found his way in here?"

"Yes, or even an Italian journalist?"

"You must be joking. Italians don't do that sort of thing," answers the first voice.

Danger over.

"Bilal, you must tell ze verity!" shouts a carabiniere. "You must tell ze verity! Ze verity, understand? If not, *bam bam*." He mimes slapping.

Verity? In English that means truth. Was it a mistake or a trap? [...]

The African girls spend the time plaiting their hair. One of them, no more than 20, has nails that are half-varnished. The upper part is embellished with a pearly glaze. The part below is unadorned. Perhaps her journey started where the varnish ends. Outside, in the small courtyard, hang the wet shoes, trousers and tops of the last ones to arrive. Yesterday evening 161 migrants landed. Then another 37. And then Bilal. There's even a Quran drying in the sun.

"Bilal" yells a voice. "You," gestures a policeman, beckoning with his hand as if to say "Follow me".

The identification office is a large room with four desks. Bilal goes to sit at the back, on the right. Facing him are two plain-clothes policemen, a computer and a youngster with a Berber face. The interpreter.

"Do you speak Arabic?" he asks, in Arabic.

"Yes," replies Bilal, also in Arabic.

"Where are you from?"

"I come from Kurdistan," says Bilal in Arabic, before switching to English. "I'd like to continue in English. Arabic is not my language. The Arabs have occupied my country."

Choosing the language of interrogation is top of the list of "migrants' rights", typed out on the prefecure's headed paper and pinned up in the corridor. A young woman joins the interrogation. She wears a US-military khaki top. All the men call her "Dottoressa" [meaning she has a university degree]. She wants to know everything. Bilal tells her he wants to go to Germany. He tells her he was locked in a container in Turkey, loaded on to a cargo ship and then boarded a motor launch a few miles from the Italian coast. Then the launch broke up. It sank. The transom couldn't support the weight of the engine. Bilal saved himself by swimming. They want to know about the Arabic text on his lifejacket.

ABOVE: Migrants picked up by Italy's Navy after being rescued in the Mediterranean Sea between the Italian and Libyan coasts, in 2014

"It says: Happiness 3. Perhaps it's the name of the ship," explains the Berber interpreter.

"Do you know what's written on it?" asks the Dottoressa in English.

Bilal answers in Arabic, looking at the interpreter. "Yes, *as-Soror talata*." And then looking at the Dottoressa: "Happiness. We all came to Europe in search of happiness."

"Good. Now we'll start the interrogation again," she announces.

Bilal has to repeat the story of his journey three times. They try to make him contradict himself. One plain-clothes agent asks him a trick question: "If you're a Kurd, do you speak Urdu?"

"No," Bilal stalls him. "Urdu is the language of Pakistan."

They ask him what he thinks of Erdoğan's government in Turkey. "No good," he replies.

They want to know what he ate on the ship. How much he paid. What was the name of the city where he was shut inside the container.

"Two weeks in a container, but how did he take a shit?" the policeman writing on the computer shouts out in Italian. The Dottoressa translates. And Bilal repeats →

→ the story he's heard countless real migrants tell.

"I peed through a hole in the metal. For the other thing, they'd take me out every two days, after it was dark. They took me to the toilet. But I never saw the ship's name. They kept my head down all the time."

They lose their rag: "*Stronzate*! Bullshit!" screams the Dottoressa. "You're telling a pack of lies. You don't come from Turkey."

Bilal feels lost. Perhaps they've guessed something. The feeling lasts just long enough for the Dottoressa to draw breath: "You've come from Libya. The Arabic on the lifejacket is the proof," she says with conviction. "Now we'll pack you off back to Gaddafi."

Another plain-clothes policeman, the largest of the lot, walks over to her. "Dottoressa," he says, continuing in Italian. "Will you leave him with us for a moment so we can take him to the torture room?"

Perhaps it is only a ruse to see if Bilal speaks Italian. To frighten him […]

After the interrogation, they take your fingerprints. Fingers and palm are pressed against the red glass of a scanner. You're automatically put on record. Outside, 21 teenagers wait their turn. They must be aged

She decides the destination of thousands who are expelled. She establishes the origin of Arab migrants by their accent

between 15 and 20. Seen like this they look like a high-school class on a school trip. But Bilal can't sit down with them. Another policeman calls him. He gives him a ticket with a registration number on it: 001. "Don't lose it," he says and hands him to the carabinieri. The military police walk up to a large green gate, swathed on all sides by hanks of barbed wire. A carabiniere opens the padlock and frees the chain. Immediately afterwards the gate swings shut again.

* * *

Immediately after sunset the police try again. The sun has already dropped, leaving a trail of spectacular colours. The agent with ice-cold eyes appears. He's with a colleague, the one who usually writes on the computer. The two of them ask the carabinieri to open the gate into the cage.

"Bilaaaal," they shout.

When Bilal arrives the policeman talks only in Italian. "Come on, we're going to interrogate you again."

It's Saturday. The day is almost over and the two of them are still at work. Bilal has to behave like a goalie at the end of the match. Hang on to the ball and kick any shots that might raise suspicions as far away as possible. In English, Bilal replies that he doesn't understand. The policeman calls the interpreter. A girl with a Moroccan accent. One he hasn't seen before. She's petite, attractive. She decides the destination of thousands who are expelled. She establishes the origin of Arab migrants by their accent.

"Do you speak English?" the policeman asks her.

"No, very little. Only Italian and Arabic," she replies.

"But this one wants to speak English," says the policeman.

"Of course, because he's Romanian. He's just taking the piss. He's not an Iraqi," answers the other man angrily.

"Go on, try and see if he really comes from Iraq then, like he claims," grumbles the policeman.

"Good evening, do you speak Arabic?" she asks Bilal in Arabic.

"Yes" is the easy answer, also in Arabic.

"What's your name and where are you from?"

It's the fourth or fifth time today that Bilal has heard the same question and he replies in broad terms. Still in Arabic. She asks him something else. But Bilal doesn't understand. At this point he'll have to test the promptness of the interpreter's reactions. All he has to do is make a vague remark and see what happens.

"*Insh'allah*." God willing, he says.

Another question he can't make out. "*Insh'allah*," repeats Bilal. And he spreads his arms like a preacher.

Another question. This time Bilal guesses the gist. He repeats in Arabic that he's from Kurdistan. That he boarded a *safina kebira*, a large ship. And now he's on Lampedusa.

Another incomprehensible question.

"Thank God, yes," he ventures. Then he says in English that because Arabic is the language of the occupation of Kurdistan, he refuses to speak Arabic and if no one on Lampedusa can speak Kurdish, then he can speak English. Bilal doesn't speak Kurdish. But neither does the interpreter.

In her rudimentary English she insists that the police want to continue in the office, not here in front of the gate. And given that Bilal can speak Arabic, the interrogation can continue in Arabic.

Replying in English, Bilal tells the girl she has beautiful eyes. It's a gamble to see if she too is bluffing. In the end neither of them knows where the conversation is going.

"I'm sorry, but I don't understand you," she apologises. "I can't interrogate you in English."

"*Bukara*," Bilal tells her after half an hour's wild goose chase through the mysteries of language.

"*Bukara*? Tomorrow? He wants to be questioned *domani*, in English," she explains to the policeman. They glance at their watches, shrug their shoulders.

"Ok, let's do it tomorrow morning with the other interpreter," says the policeman with pale eyes. "But have you found out whether he's Kurdish or Romanian at least?"

"He's not Romanian," answers the girl candidly. "He speaks very good Arabic."

The carabinieri lock the chain on the gate once again. Full marks in the practical. But is it really possible to speak a language well if you barely know 20 words? Bilal grips the bars like a monkey in the zoo as he watches the interpreter walk away. How many migrants has she sent to Libya without understanding where they came from? [...]

How many migrants has she sent to Libya without understanding where they came from?

The lavatories in the large cage on Lampedusa are an unforgettable experience. The prefabricated building is divided into two sections. In one, there are eight showers with blocked drains. Forty basins. And eight squat toilets, the hole-in-the-ground variety, of which three are brimming with a gooey substance. The other section has five toilets, two of which have no flush. Five showers. Eight basins. Salt water comes out of the taps. It's not pleasant if your skin is sunburnt, bruised and cut by the journey or riddled with scabies. The cubicles have no doors. There's no electricity. No privacy. You do everything in front of everyone. A few try to shield themselves with a towel. There's not even any toilet paper: you have to use your hands. It's better to go at night because during the day the sewage rises over the top of your slippers and your feet sink into it. [...]

Bilal needs to make a phone call. He tries the old system of opening the line with a piece of wire. But the new cardphones are protected. It doesn't work. He has an idea: the emergency number 118 is free. He tries and someone answers.

"I need help. I'm shut in the immigration centre on Lampedusa and they don't let us use the phone," he says in French. →

→ "I must let my family know. Please, if I give you an Italian number, will you ring and say that Bilal is alive. It'll cost you less than a euro."

Hundreds of fathers and sons here have the same urgent necessity. At Bilal's request, so as not to block the line, the first operator passes his call to another office.

"Do you need a doctor at the centre on Lampedusa?" asks a female medic in English.

"No, not a doctor. My family need to know that I'm alive. I'm asking you as a personal favour. Ring my family. They're in Italy. It'll cost you …"

"I'm sorry. It's not something we're required to do," says the woman and hangs up.

Bilal tries again, dialling a few freephone numbers at random. At 800-400-400 someone answers from Madre Segreta [Secret Mother], an advice bureau in the hinterland of Milan. It's a public organisation run by volunteers. They're bound to be more approachable.

"Madre Segreta, good morning," answers a girl's voice.

"Do you speak English, please?"

"Yes, I do."

Bilal tries everything. She keeps insisting that he should contact the police for this sort of thing. Bilal repeats that he's inside the cage on Lampedusa. That the police will pass the buck on to the company that runs the centre. And the company will turn the matter over to its director who's never here. He explains that the state buys phonecards – at least one when you first arrive. So even as a young volunteer, and an Italian citizen, the girl's paying for them too. But on Lampedusa the phonecards are not handed out.

"My wife's expecting a baby. If you ring this Italian number, she'll know I'm alive." Bilal almost says too much in front of the others who are listening. "Do it for my wife, please. I'm asking you a favour as one person to another. One day it might be you who needs to ask the same thing. Do you or don't you work for an organisation called Secret Mother?"

"But you're an illegal immigrant," she answers. After half an hour of trying, the girl even makes up a law: "I can't do it. The anti-terrorism law means it would be illegal for me to make the call."

"But there's no such law."

She too hangs up.

This is the worst humiliation. More painful than the beatings in the desert. More burning than the arrogance of the military police. A brutal experiment. The most chilling revelation. I hadn't asked her to give me a bed in her own home. Or even a lift in her car. Simply to make a phone call. The time it takes to say three words to a pregnant woman: Bilal is alive. How can a humane gesture be so terrifying? I feel the urge to knock down the gate. To unroll the skeins of barbed wire with my bare hands. To tear the uniforms off these mercenaries who have no power except for their own arrogance. Yet even they're not to blame. They're just kids, the same as all over the world. But what have the world's illegal immigrants done to deserve this? […] X

© Fabrizio Gatti
www.indexoncensorship.org

Translated by Lucinda Byatt

Fabrizio Gatti is an investigative journalist and the author of Bilal: Viaggiare, Lavorare, Morire Da Clandestini (Rizzoli, 2008)

HAY FESTIVAL

21–31 MAY 2015

IMAGINE THE **WORLD**

TEN DAYS OF STORIES,
IDEAS AND WONDER
WITH THE WORLD'S
GREATEST WRITERS IN
THE MOST BEAUTIFUL
L A N D S C A P E

hayfestival.org

Taking control of the camera

44(1): 17/25 | DOI: 10.1177/0306422015572972

Arts producers **Almir Koldzic** and **Áine O'Brien** look at how projects in refugee camps – from soap operas to photography classes – are giving residents the power to tell their stories

IN AN AMMAN rehearsal room are Syrian TV matinee idol Newar Bulbal, Syrian amateur actor Azmi Al Hassany, 26, and Raneen Ibraheem Aga, 23, a Syrian refugee. They are all taking part in a ground-breaking radio drama We Are All Refugees, inspired by the long-running UK radio soap opera The Archers. The refugee drama is broadcast globally on Radio Souriali, an independent Syrian station transmitted from Jordan and Syria. It is also aired in the US and via the United Nations website.

Georgina Paget, who co-produces the project with Charlotte Eagar, discusses what the project hopes to achieve: "In simple terms, the radio project aims to reach as many Syrian refugees and members of their Jordinian community as possible with dramatised presentation of topical and relevant issues about their daily lives. It aims to help all elements of the community to have a greater and deeper understanding of the situations of others living side by side with them and highlight the benefits of understanding co-operation."

The team's ambition is to gain a long-term commission for the series on either radio or television. To bolster the series' credentials they have assembled a group of established screen actors to join with refugees, co-creators and producers. The series is partly funded by the United Nations High Commissioner for Refugees, and the title We Are All Refugees has echoes of philosopher Hannah Arendt's 1943 book, We Refugees. Some 70 years later, the radio soap explores themes that now have every day and ordinary resonance, such as forced or arranged marriages for young Syrian refugee girls, domestic violence, unemployment and water shortages. It also looks at the predicament of young Syrians not allowed to work legally in Jordan and the tensions between two communities living side by side.

More than 50 million people are displaced globally, according to the UNHCR. Yet many of the images in the media are emptied of the nuanced details and the day-to-day challenges of refugee camp life.

That's why there are increasing attempts by refugee agencies and other organisations to tell refugees' stories and make their →

LEFT: A student from Do You See What I See project, Raghda, describes her photograph: "She doesn't know how, and will not have a chance, to live her childhood. It was taken away from her by the war and destruction of Syria. A child's vision in Zaatari camp is different from the vision of other children in the world. The child in camp looks toward the distant horizon, searching for a route out of this situation and looking to carry on with her life – life like other children enjoy, with play, joy, friendship"

Credit: Raghda/ Do You See What I See

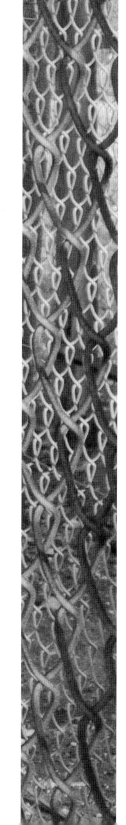

→ experiences come alive.

As the British writer, AA Gill, who won an award for his articles from refugee camps, puts it: "The hot news story is the conflict itself; this intransient, complex headache of unwanted, awkward, lumpen people doesn't have the dynamic interest of global politics or the screen-grab of smoke and bodies and Kalashnikovs."

In the Zaatari refugee camp in Jordan, for instance, a United Nations' project is working with US-based photojournalist Brendan Bannon, to equip young refugees with cameras, so they can take photos and write about their personal histories and memories. Their work has been published online and in newspapers. "We promised to give the kids a voice through photography," said Bannon. "I have heard from so many people who have seen the kids work in The New York Times and online. I am sure that the pictures are challenging preconceptions about refugee life. I hope that the work can be more widely seen in places where refugees are living today."

Alaa, 14, fled with her family from Dara'a in Syria. She now takes photos of family, friends, neighbours in Zaatari. As the family and community chronicler, she re-imagines and documents what has been lost, discover-

I am sure the pictures are changing preconceptions about refugee life. I hope that the work can be more widely seen

ing a voice through photography: "Although I'm shy," says Alaa. "I had no problem showing my work and talking about it in class. We all learned to look after each other." If she could photograph anything, it would be her house in Syria and the beautiful countryside surrounding it. "I can still remember the trees and the smell of the soil."

Lost boy found

Valentino Achak Deng *fled Sudan's civil war in the mid-1980s and started the long, treacherous walk to Ethiopia. After spending 13 years in refugee camps, he resettled in the USA, where he met best-selling writer Dave Eggers, who turned his life story into an acclaimed novel*

I had to flee from my home before I was 10 years old due to Sudan's civil war and violence in my village. Growing up in a refugee camp, I would listen to the life stories of others and share my own. Later, after resettling in the United States, I was blessed to be able to share my story with the world through the novel What is the What, which was a fictionalised account of my life by writer Dave Eggers.

When I arrived in the USA, I wanted people to know more about the war in Sudan. I wanted people to know what my people had endured. I first met Dave while he was visiting some of the "lost boys" of the Lost Boys Foundation [which helped the thousands of young refugees who had fled Sudan]. We became fast friends as he interviewed me and that started a three-year writing process. At first, I hoped to write my story myself, but realised quickly that I was not prepared to take on this task.

We were unsure of whether the biography would be in first or third person, if it would be fiction or non-fiction. Dave settled on a fictionalised biography in my voice. After the novel was a wide success in 2006, I travelled to communities around the world to speak.

On the UNHCR's Tracks website you can see refugees telling their own stories from camps or en route to sanctuary. There are experiments in immersive storytelling and the authors use photography, video and sound.

Some stories are written by journalists commissioned by the UNHCR, such as those within the Family Ties section,

I continue to speak on the importance of education, gender equality, and giving youth opportunities to lead. I have been blessed with the platform to share my life story, much by circumstance.

I hoped that by reading the novel more people would come to understand South Sudan, Sudan and Dafur. The proceeds from the book have gone to found the VAD Foundation, which created Marial Bai Secondary School in South Sudan. We now have over 400 students, and we help them move on to universities, start small businesses, meet with regional leaders, and advocate for themselves.

In recent months, I have taken a position as state minister for education in Northern Bahr el Ghazal, one of the states in South Sudan. I was tasked with the challenge of improving the primary education system and overseeing hundreds of schools working to engage our youngest citizens. It has always been my mission to give students a voice and the skills to share, clearly and passionately. The children suffer the most in times of conflict and as we rebuild a nation destroyed by decades of war, I believe they hold the future. X

Valentino Achak Deng is the co-founder and executive director of the VAD Foundation (vadfoundation.org)

charting the journeys of Syrian Kurds who find refuge with their extended families in Turkey. Istanbul-based multimedia journalist Lauren Bohn tells the story of Ibrahim: "When 41-year-old Ibrahim, one of the most cherished bread makers in the Turkish city of Suruc, heard the news that Isis was surrounding his Uncle Veysi's village near

Kobane, also known as Ayn Al Arab, he rushed to grab his mobile phone.

'I told them to get out of there right away... to come here,' he says, in the small grey courtyard of his apartment, tucked away behind his bakery just a few miles from the Syrian border. 'It's just as much their home as it is ours.'

So Veysi, his wife and children packed up as much as they could – some clothes, a

Dadaab – near the Somalian border in Kenya – is one of largest refugee camps in the world and "home" to approximately half a million people

few books and family jewellery – and fled to the border. Ibrahim, still wearing his baker's smock, was there to greet them. 'The Kurdish life in Syria, and everywhere, has always been hard,' says Veysi. 'But this is something we never imagined.'"

Stories on the Tracks website come from all over the world: from the Zaatari camp in Jordan, from Northern Iraq and the Democratic Republic of the Congo. Some are told from European makeshift camps like the ones in Pozzallo, Sicily, or Calais, France. And soon Tracks will be inviting user-generated content so the website can help create a conversation with the wider world and refugees via social media.

Another media project, Dadaab Stories, which has a lively website, is dedicated to telling stories from the enormous Dadaab refugee camp in Kenya, near the border with Somalia. Describing itself as a "collaborative community project", Dadaab Stories is an initiative run by FilmAid, which has been working in the camp screening, teaching and making films since 2006. It is funded by →

Playing with perceptions

Kate Maltby *interviews participants in Syrian Trojan Women, an acting project for refugees in Jordan*

In a shabby Amman apartment, 23-year-old Raneem has been practicing her stage make-up again. One of the 600,000 Syrian refugees living in Jordan, her clothes now come from bargain racks and charity bins, but she's still never knowingly underdressed.

For Raneem, getting her husband's permission was the hardest thing about joining the Syrian Trojan Women project. "He was worried about men seeing me, about me talking with men. But I kept going to the rehearsals because it was women I wanted to share stories with. There are things women experience in war – what it is to be a mother in war – that only they understand. I think he was jealous: he didn't come to the performance, not because he disapproved, but because he was jealous of what I had found."

Women's space or not, when Trojan Women was first performed in 415BC, it shocked, precisely because it told the truth – to men. Euripides' play was performed to an Athenian audience, shortly after the Athenian army had enslaved the entire female population of the island of Melos. "Euripides puts women's voices on stage – whoever is silently watching, those who have suffered get to confront them," says Reem, a performer and translator with the project. "Men die in wars, but women get left behind, and have to feed children and endure the chaos." Fatima, an older woman from the siege city of Homs, tells me "in school, I had heard of the Fall of Troy: but only of the men fighting, Achilles and Hector". The only woman she knew featured was Helen, the whore. "I couldn't identify with her," says Fatima. "But in Euripides' play, there are so many other women. I am Hecuba: in her own house, her palace, she knew who she was. When her house was destroyed, her identity, her dignity, was gone too."

Nobody wants to be Helen in the play. Sex, especially sex in war, isn't talked about. But whispers of rape haunt the rehearsal room: no one talks of personal experience, but everyone admits to knowing a friend's sister or cousin who has been assaulted by President Assad's enforcers. In the play when the Trojan princess Cassandra is taken into slavery, she laments her humiliation as Achilles' concubine. "When we recite Cassandra's lines," says one woman, "it's like a storm has lifted from the room." X

© Kate Maltby
www.indexoncensorship.org

Kate Maltby published a wider report on the Syrian Trojan Women project in The Times, on January 12, 2015

→ the Tribeca Film Institute New Media Fund and the Ford Foundation.

Dadaab is one of the largest refugee camps in the world and "home" to approximately half a million people. The sheer scale of Dadaab is reflected in the different generations living in the camp. As the FilmAid website puts it: "By definition, a refugee camp is temporary, but life does not stop here. Love, marriage, children, work, art – life goes on. After two decades, there are more than 8,000 Dadaab grandchildren, children of children who were born in the camp."

Unlike Tracks, which casts its storytelling net globally and across refugee camps in different countries, settlements and diaspora locations, Dadaab Stories is firmly anchored in everyday camp life. While it includes perspectives from diaspora communities, the main focus is on communications within the camp through personal videos, journalism, photography, poetry, and music. Powered

ABOVE: A young photographer from the Do You See What I See project, Mohamed Soleman, describes his picture: "Here I am thinking about how to leave the goal and defend it too so the ball does not go in"

by the social media platform, Tumblr, this is community media at its liveliest.

One of the camp's media services led by refugees and forming part of Dadaab Stories is The Refugee News, a community-run newspaper and the only local print media outlet for the population of 500,000. It is edited by a dedicated group of volunteer journalists that come from the refugee communities within the camp, with training and facilities provided by FilmAid.

By definition, a refugee camp is temporary here, but life does not stop – love, marriage, children, work, art

The Refugee News also includes a radio station called Gargaar (Somali for assistance), supported by the international non-profit, Internews, whose mission →

→ is to strengthen local media worldwide, enabling local people to circulate and hear much-needed news and information. The refugee journalists working on Radio Gargaar are all trained by Internews, with some working as professional journalists before coming to live in Dadaab.

The Syrian Trojan Women project (see box, page 20, Playing with Perceptions) for refugee women in Amman, Jordan, also co-produced by Charlotte Eagar and Georgina Paget, is using the classic Euripides anti-war tragedy to interweave drama therapy workshops, participatory storytelling and public performance, in addition to promoting understanding between refugees and host communities in Jordan. The drama workshops help refugee women who are suffering from mental anxiety, post-traumatic stress

The drama workshops help refugee women suffering from mental anxiety, post-traumatic stress, and depression

disorder, and depression. When possible, the women are paid to participate.

This relatively modest project began in 2013 with small scale workshops in Amman and has since spawned several spin-offs incluing a documentary film, titled Queens of Syria, chronicling the project's participatory methodology, and a Trojan Women tour to the US and Switzerland. Queens of Syria was shot and directed by filmmaker, Yasmin Fedaa. Fedaa engaged closely with the cast of refugee women by spending time with them in their homes and integrating the women's personal stories into the film. The aim is to screen Queens of Syria in refugee camps, at international film festivals and on television.

It is clear that we are witnessing the many ways in which photography and

Speak the speech, I pray you

Warwick University research fellow **Preti Taneja** *works on productions of Shakespeare in conflict and post-conflict situations. Here she discusses their impact*

What might Shakespeare's plays offer people forced from their homes in Syria and into a refugee camp in Jordan? Given that the pressing priorities are water, food, clothes and safety, "nothing" might be the honest answer. But that word, so central to Shakespeare's great tragedy King Lear, resonates hugely when spoken by children whose lives have been devastated by war.

In March 2014, a cast of 100 Syrian children, dressed in makeshift costumes and paper crowns, performed the play under the hot Jordanian sun. They took their places although there was no stage, just sand underfoot. Behind them, hand-painted sheets strung up on the barbed wire surrounding Zaatari, the vast camp where they live, read: "The inhabitants of Zaatari welcome the guests".

More than 60,000 children live in Zaatari, over half the total population of the camp. Shakespeare in Zaatari was a project run by Nawar Bulbul, a Syrian actor who is well known across the Arab world. Spanning a few months and, including art, theatre and writing, his project unlocked the creativity of children more used to real tragedy than playing "let's pretend". For many of them, it provided an

Credit: Muhammad Hamed/Reuters

film; the visual arts, theatre, mixed-media storytelling and online journalism are transforming the idea that refugees are voiceless victims.

As Ugandan artist Lucy Namayanja, now living in London, said: "Art can help people to come to terms with their past, to develop new perspectives and ways of dealing with

alternative to the overcrowded camp schools, which parents feel are unsafe for girls and take boys away from earning enough to help their families survive.

It is striking that Bulbul chose King Lear, and it is set in a world that has taken too little care of their needs. One of the play's most moving scenes reveals that even if a person loses all their wealth, their home and even their family, compassion for those even less fortunate remains.

Bulbul said: "The show is to bring back laughter, joy and humanity" – and not just for the children and their parents. But why Shakespeare? The name attracted global media attention. The New York Times described the scene: an audience of a few hundred people sitting on the desert ground; younger children on parents' shoulders to get a view of their siblings, watching parents beaming with pride. The performance of Shakespeare by children in this vulnerable situation served to highlight not only what they have lost, but what they could gain and offer if they had the chance.

Following the camp production, the children were invited to perform to a public audience in Jordan's Roman amphitheatre. The tagline on the poster read: "A message from the children of Zaatari to the people of the world." Such productions performed in such situations also encode a question, which the children themselves posed. "To be, or not to be?" they chanted as they left the stage. Nearly a year later, their lives remain hanging in the balance and they are still waiting for an answer from the world. ⌧

© Preti Taneja
www.indexoncensorship.org

ABOVE: Syrian children, who are living at the Zaatari refugee camp in Jordan, perform an interpretation of Shakespearean plays Hamlet and King Lear, during the Shakespeare in Zaatari event at the Roman amphitheatre in Amman, May 2014

their suffering. It certainly saved me when I was in a dark place and later on helped me expand my horizons and mind, which for years was locked in the prison of my circumstances and surroundings." ⌧

© Almir Koldzic and Áine O'Brien
www.indexoncensorship.org

Almir Koldzic and **Áine O'Brien** are co-directors of Counterpoints Arts (counterpointarts.org.uk), an arts organisation that supports, produces and promotes the arts by and about refugees and migrants. They also organise Refugee Week (15-21 June) to promote the contribution of refugees to the UK. They tweet at @CounterArts

The way I see it

44(1): 24/25 | DOI: 10.1177/0306422015572972

Two refugees living inside Palestinian refugee camps talk about how their life stories get told by others, and the reality

Outsiders think we are terrorists and uneducated

Rana Moneim

People have different views of Palestinian camps and people's lives inside them.

Outsiders often think people who live in camps have a low level of education, or they think camps are unsafe places because they are outside the control of the Lebanese government. Some imagine that life in camps is miserable. They believe people still live in tents and ancient houses.

The first thing people should know is that a large number of our young people are highly educated. They are doctors, engineers and teachers. They insist on improving themselves. They want to demonstrate that they are not lesser beings than those who live in cities and are part of the more established classes. On the contrary, they are people who are successful in their own field, but often cannot get local government jobs. So, they continue to study despite an uncertain future.

People outside the camps think that we live in tents, but this is also not correct. Some of us live in houses with all the necessary and basic needs for living. However at the same time, there are many thousands of people who live inside the camps who live in hard circumstances and need others' support.

Many people from outside the camps are scared to enter, thinking that camps are places for terrorism. We do not deny that there are plenty of troubles, often taking place because of the living conditions, but these incidents are only between individuals, and are the exception rather than the norm. It doesn't mean that camps are unsafe to live in or to visit.

But life in the camp does lack certain basic things. For example, there are no playgrounds or other means of entertainment for our children. They deserve to play and enjoy their childhood like all other children around the world. X

© Rana Moneim

Rana Moneim lives in the Rashidieh camp, Lebanon

Social media shows people how we live

Mohammed Maarouf

There was a time when the outside world had little idea of the events occurring in Palestinian camps in Lebanon. The camps stood in isolation from the surrounding cities and villages, and there was little communication with the outside world, except for rare individual relationships.

Advances in communications technology and the advent of social media has changed all that. People know what takes place inside the camps now very quickly by just looking at Whatsapp, Facebook or Twitter. Most of the local Lebanese television channels also report what happens inside the Palestinian camps and transmit the events to people all over the world.

Friends and relatives also play a significant role in publishing what is happening in camps. Most people have cousins or friends who live outside to whom they can send news or other information. Marriage

Can we be friends with the people we grew up to hate?

···

When **Rakan** *started visiting refugees in his native Lebanon, he was suprised by how it challenged his lifelong misconceptions*

The year was 1975, the drums of war echoed through every corner of the flourishing gem of Lebanon. I won't go into details of the reasons why, or who was to blame. War is a two-way dance. We are all to blame.

Christians and Palestinians went to war. There was bloodshed. Thousands died. Soldiers fed on each other's misery. The result was nil all. No one won, for in this small but highly complex country, winning a war was simply impossible.

The year is 2014. Could a Lebanese Christian be friends with a Muslim Palestinian? I thought: these are the animals my people fought. These are the people we grew up learning to hate. These are the ghosts of death that sent fear into every Christian's heart. Or was it all an illusion? And were we, Christians and Palestinians, merely actors? Was Lebanon the stage? Were we performing a script that we had no control over, written by a hidden master and directed by a foreign, deceptive director?

It was a crisp warm summer day, and the almighty yellow sun cast its rays on the southern historic Phoenician city of Tyre. I was invited into our supposed enemy's camp. I hesitantly agreed. I didn't know what to expect. How will they perceive me, an active member of a political party which not so long ago took the lives of their young people, and rendered many families without sons, daughters, mothers, and fathers?

But as soon as I entered the Palestinian camp of Rashedieh (left), all my preconceptions were shattered. The people of these camps were no enemies. They were not ghosts of death, but rather humans with the same concerns as me. They wanted to work and earn a living, with an eye on Lebanon as a safe haven, and an eye on their never-forgotten home back in holy Palestine. With open arms and accepting hearts, I was welcomed. I was truly astonished.

To this day I visit the camp at least twice a month, and the enemies of the past have turned to lifelong friends. I couldn't but sympathise with them for the living conditions they endure are not suitable for humans in this day and age. I learned a very valuable lesson – never treat a person based on preconceptions, but as brothers in humanity. If we apply this simple rule, the world can surely reign in peace. ⊠

Rakan lives in Lebanon. He wishes to remain anonymous

between Palestinians and Lebanese also facilitates communication between the inside and outside. Nowadays many students study in different universities in Lebanon or abroad, and many carry out research projects about life in the camps, again helping people better understand what's going on.

The local and international NGOs who have been working in the camps and with Palestinians, have also facilitated, enhanced and enriched the communication between Palestinians inside and outside.

The popular committees, which govern the camps, communicate on regular basis with other committees and the municipalities around the camps.

Because all these channels of communication have opened up, knowing about Palestinian camps is no longer a complicated issue. ⊠

© Mohammed Maarouf

Mohammed Maarouf lives in Rashidieh camp, Lebanon

ABOVE: Internally displaced man Sharif Afridi, 55, whose family fled the military operations in Khyber Agency, talks on his mobile phone, at the UNHCR Jalozai camp in Pakistan's northwest Khyber-Pakhtunkhwa province, April 2013

SPECIAL
REPORT

Clear connections

44(1): 27/30 | DOI: 10.1177/0306422015570521

Refugees are using technology to
stay in touch with their families
despite being thousands of miles
away, but there are security risks,
Jason DaPonte reports

"MY WIFE CHANGES her sim card
every week," said Omid, an Iranian
refugee who hasn't seen his wife in the seven
years he has been awaiting a decision in his
UK asylum case. The couple use Viber, a
mobile app that allows free voice calls over
the internet, but his wife remains in constant
fear of surveillance. Omid is wanted by the
Iranian state for political offences. He's also a
convert to Christianity and his wife fears discussing his new religion, as even members of
his own family have branded him an infidel.

Refugees may be some of the most excluded people in society, but social media and
new technology nevertheless play a crucial
role in many of their lives. Across the globe,
refugees are finding ways of using them to
stay connected to families, homelands and
political causes, in ways they couldn't have
a decade ago – even though it can have security implications. A number of refugees,
particularly from Syria, suggested they use
the free messaging mobile app, WhatsApp,
because they believe the messages are secure.
Whether WhatsApp messages can be hacked
or intercepted is not clear, however.   →

ABOVE: Palestinian boys play in a computer game shop in the Palestinian Beddawi refugee camp in northern Lebanon, May 2007

→ Ismail Einashe, a British journalist and Africa expert, originally from Somaliland, explained another way social media is changing the refugee experience (Einashe also writes for this issue; see Escape From Eritrea, Volume 44, 1/2015). He said how his teenage cousin, who fled Somaliland for Austria, uses Facebook for photo-sharing, to craft an image of success and happiness. But this can potentially hide the true difficulties of refugee life.

"My cousin is inspired by American hip-hop. He wears baseball caps and baggy jeans – so his friends at home see the glamorous 'other' and they don't see the high unemployment or poverty among refugees. It's partly encouraging the young generation. Before, people didn't see what life on the other side could be and now they can see it," he told Index.

Nearly every refugee interviewed for this article said that free calls on Skype and the ability to connect with relatives for free using standard social platforms (like Facebook) is invaluable to them. But for some, sharing stories from exile goes beyond simple messaging and status updates. Some refugees use blogs and social media channels to publish content banned at home to try to fight the repression they escaped.

Moses Walusimbi fled Uganda's anti-gay laws for The Netherlands and now runs Uganda Gay On Move – a blog, Facebook and Twitter movement that helps gay Ugandans and Africans who have fled persecution, as well as providing information for those who are left behind and remain under threat.

"When I came to Holland, I realised the more you keep quiet the more you suffer," Walusimbi told Index. "I was very eager to know if there were any other Ugandans who are in Holland who are like me, in the same situation. And when I started these social media things, many Ugandans responded."

His movement now has almost 9,000 followers on Facebook, which he says is the most popular platform for his content. He also has followers on Twitter and his blog. Uganda Gay On Move is providing a support network that goes beyond publishing, with many photos of meetings between its members for social and political reasons.

"Uganda Gay On Move is like a family to us now. It's like a family because we come together, we discuss, we find solutions," said Walusimbi. These solutions have included the group petitioning and lobbying the Dutch parliament to raise awareness about the denial of the human rights of gay Ugandans and other Africans. It also publishes information that helps asylum-seekers manage their cases and gather evidence. But Walusimbi still worries about those in Uganda who could face jail sentences simply for reading it.

"Ugandan LGBTI people – unless well known human rights defenders – tend to use false names on Facebook. There is also a danger when people attend internet cafes and do not securely log off. There is also a danger – and I have had several direct reports of family or friends seeing the Facebook pages left open on computers in homes. Some people have been exposed this way," Melanie Nathan, an LGBTI activist and publisher who has worked closely with African LGBTI movements, told Index. "Using Facebook could result in meetings or revealing real names through trust and then in entrapment." Walusimbi corroborated that there are real cases where this has happened.

Blogs by and for refugees from various conflict zones are building audiences. The Medeshi Somaliland blog is one example. It was founded with a desire to keep in touch with a dispersed family and diaspora in 2007 by Mo Ali, who left Somaliland to seek asylum in the UK in 2004. His work of aggregating and creating new content quickly became more political.

"There are many websites about Somaliland and those who are publishing there have been harassed by the police. They've been ordered to shut down because of being critical of the government on freedom of speech and press," Ali told Index, saying he knows of at least three websites that have been shut down and explaining why he has to publish from abroad.

Some refugees use blogs and social media channels to publish content banned at home to try to fight the repression they escaped

Even publishing from the UK, he doesn't feel totally safe, "I've received death threats via email but I published the threat online and nothing happened. I'm still alive. It was just intimidation."

Like Uganda Gay On Move, Ali has used the blog's following to campaign, and in 2010 and 2012 rallied more than 1,000 of his followers to lobby outside London's Parliament for official recognition of Somaliland.

Refugees are working on their own and with professional content and software creators to find bespoke ways to tell their stories. Dadaab Stories and the related Refugee News are two of the most elegant →

→ projects that have used the power of free social media tools (particularly Tumblr and YouTube) to help refugees publish stories. In these cases, professional filmmakers and refugees worked together to create ongoing social media coverage of the refugee camp for Somalians in Kenya.

Globally available and free technology platforms are helpful, but tools, platforms and projects are now emerging that are specifically aimed at refugees to allow them to self-organise and connect digitally.

Refunite is a social network designed to connect dispersed families that have low access to technology following displacement. It allows refugees to remain anonymous to everyone other than their family members, which aids those who may not be able to register with formal institutions because they are awaiting asylum decisions or are stateless. The platform currently reaches more than 500,000 refugees and is aiming to connect 1 million during 2015. It is geared towards low-end mobile technology to ensure that nearly anyone can use it. It can even be accessed using an interactive voice response system or text-messaging for those who are illiterate or don't have internet access.

Low-cost and low-barrier-to-entry technologies such as these are proving to be a key part of connecting refugees in crisis. The UNHCR is telling the world the story of Jordan's Zaatari camp via Twitter (which has claimed to be the first refugee camp with an official Twitter account). Nasreddine Touaibia, a UNHCR communications associate at the camp described how WhatsApp, a free or low-cost mobile messaging system, is being used by Syrian refugees to self-organise. "Urgent messages are sent to these groups and they are reflected in the Facebook group later. It's their own emergency broadcast network," he told Index, describing how WhatsApp had been used to give warnings when flooding occurred at the camp.

South African technology startup Vumi is now trying to build on this trend of using low-cost messaging services to create technical products that can empower refugees to self-organise at scale. Its platform uses mass mobile messaging and low-fi browsing to enable access to civic information.

Building on its success in Libya of technically enabling Wikipedia Zero (a Wikipedia Foundation project which gives access to Wikipedia without data charges in 35 countries) and distributing voter information, the company is now in the planning stages for a project focussed on empowering refugees, in partnership with South Africa's Lawyers for Human Rights, an NGO that deals largely with refugees in South Africa.

Various NGOs and other services are also using social media to provide platforms that help refugees re-settle. These are largely regionally based and aim to help refugees understand the legal and social contexts they are in. In the UK, the Refugee Council and Bail for Immigration Detainees provide online resources and tools that help refugees build and understand their legal cases. Migrant Voice, another UK-based organisation, provides training and tools to allow migrants (including refugees) to publish and communicate their stories.

Refugees and migrants certainly benefit from the uses of social media that everyone with internet access does; but the emerging platforms in the space are where the traditional model of solitary, isolated migrants can be disrupted. Tools specifically tailored to the needs of the excluded have the potential to create the most significant change in a networked world. ◻

© Jason DaPonte
www.indexoncensorship.org

Additional reporting by Ibrahim Zanta

Jason DaPonte is the former editor of BBC mobile and founder of The Swarm. He tweets @jasondap

Who tells the stories?

44(1): 31/33 | DOI: 10.1177/0306422015570562

Mary Mitchell writes on the project she co-founded at a Lebanese camp for Palestinian refugees to help share their own experiences

AS A STORYTELLER, I can no longer say with quite the same confidence: "This is not political. Tell me about your mother, your love, your family, your hobbies, your food." New approaches to the documentary genre are transforming the way in which stories are told from refugee camps, shifting the role of the outsider from teller to catalyst, from speaker to listener, and from writer to trainer and facilitator, resulting in first-hand stories of resilience, survival and pain.

In October 2014, I began a storytelling project in one of Lebanon's Palestinian refugee camps, Al Rashidiya, which has profoundly challenged the way I view communication, voice and listening. Internet access and social media usage have provoked questions in marginalised communities around the world, such as "who gets to tell the story?" and "how is it told?", and Humans of Al Rashidiya is a response to this, attempting to provide a platform for storytelling by, for and from a community with few digital resources or social capital.

Humans of Al Rashidiya is inspired by the popular Humans of New York project, which accompanies photos of passers-by on the streets of New York with short, often intimate, text about their lives. Using the same format to encourage sharing, commenting and the repurposing of images, we shared one story per day from the camp during the months of October and November, creating a platform for people in the camp to submit stories. Although the daily photo sharing has

stopped, the live page continues to gather comments from people all over the world.

The stories – shared on Facebook and Tumblr – are about everything from love and family life to unemployment and maintaining culture in the diaspora. Amid touching stories about the journey into exile and the struggles faced by Palestinians from Syria (now twice displaced) are stories of anger and frustration – and of simply getting on with life.

As Mohammed Al Assad, the co-director, and I were walking through the camp one day in September we found Abu Nabil, a resident in his early 70s, sitting outside his home. I wanted Abu Nabil to tell me something about love and marriage. Instead he wanted to talk about the injustice of the difference between our lives. He said: "It's a difficult life here in the camps. We are far from our land. Your life in England is not like our life here because you have a house in your own country. We are out of Palestine, you can see how we live here, it's very difficult, not like your life, or anybody who has his own house in his own country. This life is very, very difficult. If I could live in my own house, my own building in my own country, then life would be not difficult for us." He died a few weeks later.

The second stage of the project involves collaboration with a youth group in the camp, where a team of young people will be trained in digital storytelling, filmmaking, blogging and social media, creating →

ABOVE: Nahla Bader, one of the participants in Humans of Al Rashidiya: "Someone came in the night [when she was 8 years old] and said on a loudspeaker that King Hussein said all the Palestinians in Aqqa must leave within 24 hours. Before my mother-in-law died she asked some foreign people who came to visit Rashidiya to go to Aqqa to get some soil. They found an old Jewish man on her land. When they told him that the owner of the land is still alive and she wants a bag of soil from her land he started crying and filled two bags of soil to give to her. I miss my house, the land and the ground for planting. When I go to the border, I can smell the air from Palestine"

→ content for an interactive documentary to be broadcast on Facebook.

The cafe operated by this youth group has the last line of the London-based Palestinian poet Rateef Ziadah's spoken word piece, We Teach Life, Sir, painted on the wall, as a reminder of the uneven power balance of mainstream media and how the pain of human experience is condensed into an outsider's agenda. It reads: "Today, my body was a TV'd massacre that had to fit into soundbites and word limits and move those that are desensitised to terrorist blood."

Communication from inside refugee camps has historically been the preserve of journalists, advocates and aid workers rather than those who have been displaced, and stories have therefore revolved solely around outsiders' objectives. The stories and questions being shared and raised by those engaging with Humans of Al Rashidiya are crucial to changing this dominance.

New technological capabilities and social media platforms make everyone a storyteller and challenge the notion that only those with expensive equipment and connections to editors can tell a story. As this assumption continues to shift, Humans of Al Rashidiya and others projects like it are enabling marginalised communities to share stories of survival rather than victimhood, and agency rather than passivity. ☒

© Mary Mitchell
www.indexoncensorship.org

Mary Mitchell is a PhD student at Royal Holloway University of London. She has worked in international development and in charity communications

"I think about when I will be a human with rights"

Mohammed Al Assad, *a student and co-director Humans of Al Rashidiya, was born in the Lebanese camp*

I was born in Al Rashidiya and I have grown up, played and studied in the schools of this camp. It's beautiful to live in such a tightly knit community with people from different families, but the beauty is constantly undermined by the pain of the people's suffering. Living at the Palestinian camps in Lebanon means isolation and a suppression of freedoms. All the camps have borders, and each exit and entrance to the camp has an army checkpoint, where guards ask to see your personal ID, ask where you're going and where you come from.

In Al Rashidiya, there is a feeling among the youth of being isolated from Lebanese societies, the West and the wider Arab world. The isolation from Lebanese society is a legacy of the conflict between the Lebanese armed forces and Fatah al-Islam in Nahr al-Bared camp in 2007, and religious differences between the two communities.

Many Lebanese people think the camps are dangerous and it's too dangerous to enter them, and many think the people in the camps are different from them. There is a common prejudice that Palestinian refugees are not educated and are responsible for crime in the areas surrounding the camps.

Those of us who live in the camps know we are humans with rights and intelligence, and our potential is the same as that of anyone else. Al Rashidiya is full of educated people who don't have the right to be employed, and there is a high success rate in our schools.

I'm fearful for myself and for all Palestinians in this situation. I am worried about the future – that when I finish my university studies I will not find a job and will have to emigrate like many other people from the camp. I think all the time about when I will be a human with rights, land, safety and security. It's hard not to if you are born a Palestinian in Lebanon.

Nowadays our society is starting to open up to other societies, both near and far, through technology and youth activism. I am co-directing the Humans of Al Rashidiya project to help ease the isolation of the camps by sharing daily stories from and by Palestinians in the camps on Facebook and Tumblr. We focus on groups of people who don't often have their voices heard, such as the elderly and the youth.

It's difficult to be a child here because there are so few opportunities. You are told to work hard in school, but then you graduate and realise that there are no jobs. We want to bring out the voices of these children and the frustrations of the youth.

Although our families have been exiled from our country for nearly 70 years, we will never forget the right to return, and it is our job to communicate our existence to the outside world. X

© Mohammed Al Assad
www.indexoncensorship.org

ABOVE: A street in Al Rashidiya refugee camp, 2014

Mohammed Al Assad is from Al Rashidiya camp in Lebanon. His grandparents sought refuge in Lebanon in 1948. He is a student at the Lebanese German University

Realities of the promised land

44(1): 34/37 | DOI: 10.1177/0306422015571092

After Haiti's devastating earthquake, Brazil opened its doors to immigrants seeking new opportunities. Five years on, **Iara Beekma** reports from inside the camps for new arrivals and looks at fears of immigrant workers being silenced into slavery

SERGO PIERRE LOUIS is one of an estimated 30,000 Haitians who have travelled down the Americas by plane, bus and foot to reach Brazil. He and many others left Haiti in the aftermath of the earthquake that devastated their homeland in January 2010. A former civil engineer, he now works at a fast-food restaurant in the south-eastern Brazilian state of São Paulo. "Things are much worse for Haitians than those we left behind in our country can imagine," he said. "I have been working at a fast-food restaurant for the past seven months without getting paid. My only option is to find a job in a different place. What can I do? Who can I complain to?"

Five years ago, Brazil's president, Dilma Rouseff, opened the country's doors to Haitians. The federal government established an official camp for the migrants in Brasiléia, a remote town in the north-west state of Acre, bordering Bolivia to its southwest and only 100km from Peru. In the first year, the town hosted 37 Haitian refugees, but this rapidly swelled to 1,175 in 2011, 2,225 in 2012, 10,779 in 2013, and 13,047 in 2014, according to the federal police.

Haitian immigrants are not officially considered refugees under Brazilian law, which only terms people suffering from persecution related to race, religion, nationality or political reasons under the UN's 1951 convention on refugees. However, Brazil has welcomed Haitians on humanitarian grounds and for the boost they give to the labour market as the economy swells. Haitians, in turn, are determined to get to Brazil as they believe there are better job opportunities there. What they don't foresee is working for no pay and being afraid to speak out.

Brazil's need for manual labour has turned the camp into a goldmine for private companies. Carlos Cesar Ferreira de Souza, a camp employee, said: "There is not enough manpower in the camp to fill the demand of companies. On one hand, this is good for the refugees, but the problem comes once they realise that they will be making minimum wage for intense manual labour." Many Haitian migrants, he said, have been led to believe they will make at least $3,000 a month so there is a bad mismatch between the reality and their expectations.

Part of the refugees' desperation comes from the fact they have endured a long, hazardous journey just getting to Brazil. In theory, all visas for migrants should be issued from the Brazilian embassy in Haiti, but the office is hugely overworked. One

ABOVE: Haitian immigrants at the old Brazilian camp in Brasiléia, Acre. Overcrowding caused the camp to be shutdown in April 2014

Haitian told The New Yorker magazine, in August last year, that getting an appointment was "like winning the lottery". So many take the riskier route. They fly direct to Ecuador, where an entry visa is not required, then continue overland either through the Peruvian or Bolivian Amazon until they reach Brazil. Along the way, many fall prey to *coiotes* (people traffickers). Women can also find themselves sexually abused.

"I witnessed everything you can imagine [on the overland journey to Brazil]," one Haitian immigrant, Finette Sensuel, told Index. "But because I speak Spanish I could defend myself. Unlike most women, I escaped sexual abuse, making me one of the lucky few. The worst part is not having anyone to turn to. Without papers, we have no right to complain."

The worst part is not having anyone to turn to. Without papers, we have no right to complain

Now the journey to a refugee camp in Brazil has become even longer. The original camp in Brasiléia was forced to shut →

→ down in April 2014 because of severe overcrowding. A press exposé showed refugees living in inhumane and severely unhygienic conditions. After the closure, the state government opened a new camp the same month, 230km further from the Bolivian-Brazilian border at Rio Branco, Acre's state capital. Facilities certainly improved. More than 20 bathrooms were built as well as a medical centre, but the extra distance from the border added further obstacles for migrants. Carlos Portela, a local activist, said he knew of people who were intercepted at the Brazilian-Peruvian border and given fake documents, saying their entry had been denied. In despair they had fallen into the hands of people traffickers.

There is great relief that comes from finally registering at the camp. The process of moving from being an undocumented Haitian immigrant to obtaining a work permit and "humanitarian visa" usually takes no more than five days. As one Haitian resident,

Haitian migrants are taking over manual labour jobs in Brazil. But if we do not act quickly, Brazil will become a market for slavery

Lucner Rosemin, said: "Even though this is far from the Brazil I hoped for, the people from Brasiléia have been hospitable. When I got sick, the head of the camp, Damiao Borges, immediately took me to the hospital, where I had the same rights as any other Brazilian. The nurse who treated me still invites me over for lunch every Sunday with her family."

A spokesperson for the Norwegian Refugee Council, which works with migrants all over the world, told Index: "Refugees can often only find work in the informal economy. By its very nature the informal sector is

|||||||||||||||||||||||||||||||||||||||||||||||||||||

I am no longer homeless, but I work without pay

Sergo Pierre Louis, a civil engineer, gave up his job in Haiti to seek a better life in Brazil, but he has found himself exploited with nowhere to turn for help

It was early on 19 February last year when I decided to leave Haiti and all my belongings behind, as well as my job as a civil engineer. I sold everything that was in my name and managed to travel down to Brazil – first setting foot in Brasiléia.

Of course I thought I would quickly recover my investment, but that is far from the case. I have no one to turn to. My complaints all go unheard and merely threaten to worsen my situation.

More than seven months have gone by since I left the camp in Brasiléia and was taken in by my *chefe* (boss) to work at a fast-food restaurant in São Paulo, where I am given a meal a day and a place to sleep as a form of compensation. Sometimes I work more than 12-hour shifts, yet I have not a single [Brazilian] real in my pocket.

The few times I complained and asked my boss for some money, he reminded me that he picked me off the streets. It is true, I was homeless at the time. He was the only person who gave me a place to stay, but only to be at his disposal at all times. It is not worth complaining to the Ministry of Labour, I will only lose my job. At the same time I am also thankful to my *chefe*; my situation before was far worse than the one I am in now.

Maybe it is not fair to have expected so much of Brazil, but I was hoping for something more than I left behind. I just hope that the Haitians who are still coming this way are fortunate enough to find hospitable people along the way – as I did. But, I also wish that the conditions to receive them improve and they are not disillusioned. X

© Sergo Pierre Louis
www.indexoncensorship.org

Based on an interview with Iara Beekma

unregulated, making it an ideal space for unscrupulous employers to exploit and traffic workers. The incidence in Brazil with Haitian refugees should not be considered as isolated."

One year ago, the Central Única dos Trabalhadores (CUT), Brazil's main trade union, declared its solidarity with the Haitian refugees in the country, requesting that public policy specifically protects the rights of both immigrants and refugees in Brazil. Progress on Haitian workers' rights is slow but small steps are being made to improve their condition. In March, the camp is establishing a partnership with the Ministry of Social Development to teach migrants Portuguese, so they can better stand up for themselves.

And yet still the stories of exploitation emerge. In August 2014, 12 Haitian refugees were discovered working at a sewing workshop, receiving housing and board as a form of payment for up to 15 hours' work per day. Brazil's Ministry of Labour has confirmed that the number of refugees in these conditions is increasing and it's an issue they are trying to control.

"Haitian migrants are taking over manual labour jobs in Brazil. But if we do not act quickly, Brazil will become a market for slavery," says Carlos Cesar Ferreira de Souza, an employee at the camp in Acre state. "Even though we run a back-up check on companies before we allow them to come to the camp, we have no system to truly verify what occurs once refugees leave our grounds." ☒

© Iara Beekma
www.indexoncensorship.org

Iara Beekma lives in her home country, Bolivia, where she is concluding her thesis at Utrecht University on the Haitian and Senegalese migration to Brazil through the Peruvian and Bolivian borders

The whole picture

44(1): 38/42 | DOI: 10.1177/0306422015571886

Magnum photographer **Chris Steele-Perkins** has spent decades covering refugee camps around the world. He reports on the challenges he, and other photographers, face getting stories right

IN **1994 I** was in Uganda trying, rather unsuccessfully, to do a story on the traditional kings of Uganda, when I heard a report on the BBC World Service about the exodus of ethnic Hutus from Rwanda across the border into what was then Zaire, at a crossing point near the town of Goma. It sounded incredible: tens of thousands of people were crossing on foot with no idea of what awaited them.

Earlier in the year, the Hutu tribal majority had perpetrated genocide on the minority Tutsi people. Neighbour turned on neighbour, friend on friend, killing squads were organised, and over 100 days it is estimated that between half a million and one million people were murdered. The intervention of the rebel Tutsi army (RPF) turned the tables so that the Hutu, fearing retribution, started to flee.

From Uganda the journey to the refugee camp was fraught with problems. There was a 560km drive across difficult terrain. We had to confront drunken soldiers, pay out bribes and navigate poor roads.

I thought when I covered the famine and civil war in Somalia in 1992 that I had seen the lower reaches of hell. I did not realise there were even lower depths. Goma was worse than Somalia and the scale was staggering. Once the border was opened people were funnelled over a narrow bridge into town, carrying whatever they could with them, including their children. They walked over a carpet of bodies of those that had died on the bridge. There was no other way in.

Once in town, much of which had been wrecked by previous fighting, people lay down wherever they could on the sharp skin-slicing volcanic pumice that dominated the landscape. NGO workers hunted through the people, distributing water, transferring the worst cases to make-shift clinics and feeding centres. Abandoned children, and those who had lost their parents, or whose parents had died, wandered around like ghosts. The smaller ones sat and cried.

Some who were stronger were encouraged to keep going a few kilometres beyond Goma to larger camps in the countryside, where they would get food rations and materials to construct a shelter.

The corpses literally piled up in the street. Some were bulldozed into mass graves. When local residents protested by making a roadblock of corpses, the Zairean army turned up and ordered them to be moved, and then went away again. Women filled water pots from the lake where bloated bodies floated yards away. Scavengers took clothes from stinking bodies. Children died in front of me. Some aid organisations were making heroic efforts to help the displaced people but the overriding sense was one of sleepwalking through madness. How to convey this nightmare? I think I failed. →

ABOVE: Rwandan refugees in Goma, Zaire (now Democratic Republic of the Congo), in 1994

ABOVE: Women take a sewing class in a camp in the Nadir region, Burma, in 2014

Credit: Chris Steele-Perkins / Magnum

→ In those pre-digital days a major logistical issue was how to get my film out of the country. The Red Cross had a number of small planes bringing in staff and supplies from Nairobi. I arranged for a pilot to take some film from me, and for him to contact my agency, Magnum, so the film could be transported to Paris. However, the pilot forgot and put my unprocessed film in his locker room and went on holiday for a week. When the film got back to Europe it was two weeks late.

How easy it was to feel sorry for myself and lose perspective. The fragile journalist's ego bruised while my subjects lay under a

raging sun. I had lost 14 days of not being on the front pages. They were losing their children, their health, their homes, their sanity.

How beguiling the country could be too. Early in the morning, before the sun rose, and the stench invaded your pores, it was beautiful: pools of low mist, the glow of fires, smoke drifting, fluid abstract bodies balancing baskets and goods in silhouette against a waxing sky. This was the visual fodder of tourist brochures conjured from the landscape of suffering.

It is easy to be judgemental, far too easy. How often did I find myself thinking of the Hutu refugees: "Did you butcher your neighbours? Is that *panga* [machete] you're carrying stained with human blood?" I even thought: "They deserve this after what they have done!" But not all are guilty. There are the children. They are the innocent. Justice, if there ever is justice, follows another course. That kind of thinking puts me on the level of the killers and I had to ask myself if I could ever do what some of them had done. The answer for us all is hard to accept, but we know that there are circumstances in which we could have.

Shortly after I got home from Zaire I became ill. I could hardly get out of bed or feed myself. I dragged myself to the Hospital for Tropical Diseases in London and had some tests. They found I was suffering from shock. I was sent home to lie down and rest. I had thought myself invulnerable but I had not been able to go through those experiences without being marked.

Almost two decades later I covered the Rohingya refugee situation in Burma. It was a totally different experience. The Rohingya, originally Bangladeshi Muslims, had never been given Burmese nationality and had been the target of violence by the local Arkanese population at various times. In 2013 the Rohingya had again been attacked in serious numbers and many driven from their homes. Some were now in makeshift camps, some in purpose-built camps and some were re-settled in areas with a high Rohingya population that had remained free of attacks.

Access to some of the camps was very easy, while others, the more inadequate ones, I was told, required government permission which I did not have time to get. So I flew to Sittwe where the nearest camps were close to town. Normally the United Nations and NGOs are happy to help visiting journalists, but the government control was such that they were paranoid about having their operations closed down if they were seen to be working with us.

Fortunately I had been in touch with Aung Win before I left London, a fluent English speaker who had become somewhat of a press spokesman for the Rohingya. He and his family were displaced and he now lived in a house within a local Rohingya area, just outside Sittwe which had remained unscathed by violence. I took a taxi to the edge of the community, passed a laid-back police post, and was met by Aung Win and a 4×4 he had arranged for transport. The camps did not appear until we had driven about 30 minutes to Nazir district where we got to a metal bridge and looking down from the bridge to the right, the camp was pointed out to me. It had become an extension of

I remember being outraged in El Salvador by US crews pushing their cameras into grieving people's faces. But, because I stood further back, did that make me superior?

the existing village. Some of the houses were constructed of tin and plastic. Others were just like village dwellings, small wood and straw houses with bits of polythene patching. The area was poor, but not exceptional. Some local women had started a sewing class to help provide a source of income. Neighbours stood and chatted, put washing out to dry on plants, and children climbed trees.

Deeper inland were some purpose-built camps, such as Baw Du Pha, with regimented rows of rooms and a numbering system like a barracks. Nearby an enterprising farmer had hired some land and was running a successful melon farm. It was clear that the people here were not going back to their homes any time soon. This was now their home.

Aung Win explained the underlying neglect, and discrimination practised by the government. He explained how a hospital had been closed in Dapaing village, a →

→ Muslim enclave, as doctors no longer came and there was no medicine. A local nurse and a midwife from the camps kept watch at the hospital so they could at least provide advice to those patients who came expecting help. They did not want to be photographed for fear of reprisals.

The government had withdrawn funding to these areas, so in most places schools were run by volunteer teachers who were dedicated young people, mostly women. In the mosques, which were often just a tin-roofed platform, Quranic classes were held. In the village of Thea Chaung, where a number of refugees had gathered we saw a young imam trying to control lively kids, excited by the appearance of a strange photographer. There had been other photographers, film crews, journalists, and fact-finding missions before me, Aung Win said. He had taken about 150 journalists to visit the mosque, enquire, film and then move on.

How should we as journalists conduct ourselves in these situations? I remember being outraged in El Salvador by US television crews who were, as I saw it, pushing their cameras into people's faces as they grieved. But, because I stood further back, did that make me superior? I was not invisible. I was still invading their grief and converting it to foreign currency, selling my work by recording their heartbreak. Nowadays I try to explain to people who I am, seek their agreement and try to communicate with them, if not in words, then by touch, gesture, a smile or movement of the head: the body language of empathy. And the photographer's role is one of empathy. Without an emotional connection how can the photographer expect the audience to connect? But, at the same time, you're a professional, you have to deliver, you cannot indulge in sentiment.

As in Goma, so in Sittwe, I try to do my best, but it all feels so inadequate in the balance of things when my home has not been destroyed, when my family has been killed,

when I have not been rejected by the government of the county I live in. I can leave the confines of the refugee camps, drive past the laid-back police post, and take a plane to my comfortable home and consider if I want my chateaubriand steak medium or rare. X

© Chris Steele-Perkins
www.indexoncensorship.org

Chris Steele-Perkins is a Magnum photographer. His books include Fading Light and Northern Exposures, both published by McNidder and Grace

The Stephen Spender Prize

for poetry in translation 2015

Translate a poem from any language, ancient or modern, into English

Cash prizes • winning entries published in a booklet • details and entry forms at www.stephen-spender.org • closing date Friday 22 May 2015

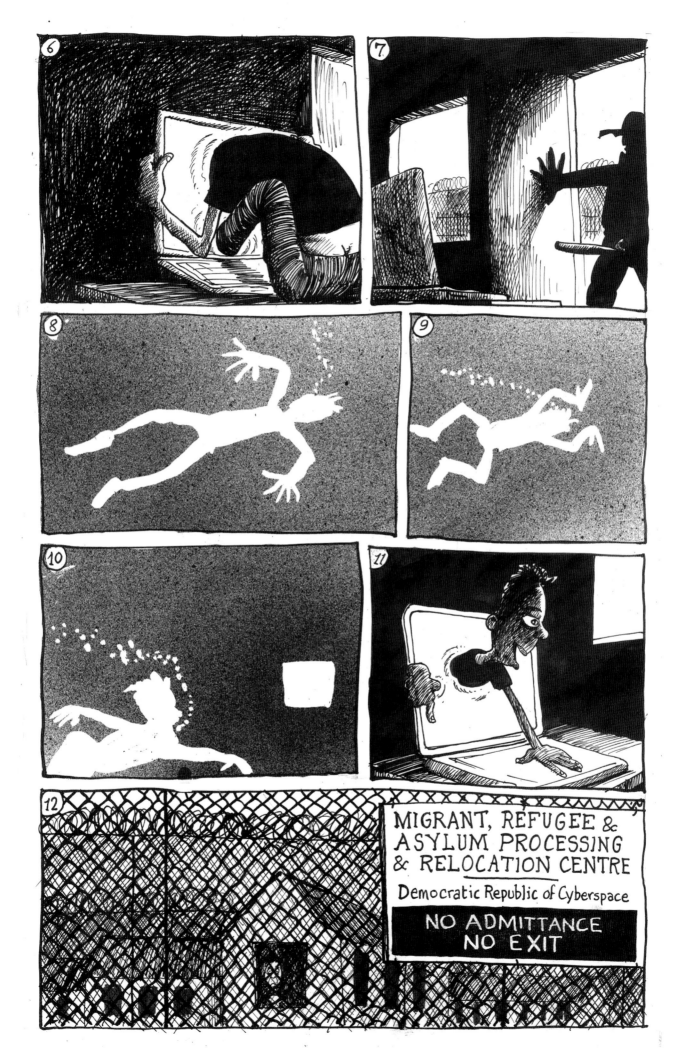

Escape from Eritrea

44(1): 46/49 | DOI: 10.1177/0306422015570783

As refugees flee one of the world's most repressive and secretive regimes, **Ismail Einashe** talks to Eritreans who have reached the UK but who still worry about the risks of speaking out

TELEVISION JOURNALIST TEMESGHEN Debesai had waited years for an opportunity to make his escape, so when the Eritrean ministry of information sent him on a journalism training course in Bahrain he was delighted, but fearful too. On arrival in Bahrain, he quietly evaded the state officials who were following him and got in touch with Reporters Sans Frontières. Shortly after he met officials from the United Nations High Commissioner for Refugees who verified his details. He then went into hiding for two months so the Eritrean officials in Bahrain could not catch up with him and eventually escaped to Britain.

Debesai told no one of his plans, not even his family. He was concerned he was being watched. He says a "state of paranoia was everywhere" and there was no freedom of expression. Life in Eritrea, he explains, had become a "psychological prison".

After graduating top of his class from Eritrea's Asmara University, Debesai became a well-known TV journalist for state-run news agency Erina Update. But from 2001, the real crackdown began and independent newspapers such as Setit, Tsigenai, and Keste Debena, were shut down. In raids journalists from these papers were arrested en masse. He suspects many of those arrested were tortured or killed, and many were never heard of again. No independent domestic news

agency has operated in Eritrea since 2001, the same year the country's last accredited foreign reporter was expelled.

The authorities became fearful of internal dissent. Debesai noticed this at close hand having interviewed President Afwerki on several occasions. He describes these interviews as propaganda exercises because all questions were pre-agreed with the minister of information. As the situation worsened in Eritrea, the post-liberation haze of euphoria began to fade. Eritrea went into lock-down. Its borders were closed, communication with the outside world was forbidden, travel abroad without state approval was not allowed. Men and women between the ages of 18 and 40 could be called up for indefinite national service. A shoot-to-kill policy was put in operation for anyone crossing the border into Ethiopia.

Debesai felt he had no other choice but to leave Eritrea. As a well-known TV journalist he could not risk walking across into Sudan or Ethiopia, so he waited until he got the chance to leave for Bahrain.

Eritrea was once a colony of Italy. It had come under British administrative control in 1941, before the United Nations federated Eritrea to Ethiopia in 1952. Nine years later Emperor Haile Selassie dissolved the federation and annexed Eritrea, sparking Africa's longest war. This long bitter war →

ABOVE: An Eritrean family in a refugee camp

→ glued the Eritrean people to their struggle for independence from Ethiopia. Debesai, whose family went into exile to Saudi Arabia during the 1970s, returned to Eritrea as a teenager in 1992, a year after the Eritrean People's Liberation Front captured the capital Asmara.

For Debesai returning to Asmara had been a "personal choice". He wanted to be a part of rebuilding his nation after a 30-year conflict, and besides, he says, life in postwar Asmara was "socially free", a welcome antidote to conservative Saudi life. Those heady days were electric, he says. An air of "patriotic nationalism" pervaded the country. Women danced in the streets for days welcoming back EPLF fighters. Asmara had remained largely unscathed during the war thanks to its high mountain elevation. Much of its beautiful 1930s Italian modernist architecture was intact, something Debesai was delighted to see.

Debesai was concerned he was being watched. He says a "state of paranoia was everywhere" and there was no freedom of expression

But those early signs of hope that greeted independence quickly soured. By 1993 Eritreans overwhelmingly voted for independence, and since then Eritrea has been run by President Isaias Afwerki, the former rebel leader of the EPLF. Not a single election has been held since the country gained independence, and today Eritrea is one of the world's most repressive and secretive states. There are no opposition parties and no independent media. No independent public gatherings or civil society organisations are permitted. Amnesty International estimates there are 10,000 prisoners of conscience in Eritrea, who include journalists, critics, dissidents, as well as men and women who

have evaded conscription. Eritrea is ranked the worst country for press freedoms in the world by Reporters Sans Frontières.

The only way for the vast majority of Eritreans to flee their isolated, closed-off country is on foot. They walk over the border to Sudan and Ethiopia. The United Nations says there are 216,000 Eritrean refugees in Ethiopia and Sudan. By the end of October 2014, Sudan alone was home to 106,859 Eritrean refugees in camps at Gaderef and Kassala in the eastern, arid region of the country.

In Ethiopia, Eritrean refugees are found mostly in four refugee camps in the Tigray region, and two in the Afar region in north-eastern Ethiopia.

During the first 10 months of 2014, 36,678 Eritreans sought refuge across Europe, compared to 12,960 during the same period in 2013. Most asylum requests were to Sweden (9,531), Germany (9,362) and Switzerland (5,652). The UN says the majority of these Eritrean refugees have arrived by boat across the Mediterranean. The majority of them are young men, who have been forced into military conscription. All conscripts are forced to go to Sawa, a desert town and home to a military camp, or what Human Rights Watch has called an open-air prison. Many young men see no way out but to leave Eritrea. For them, leaving on a perilous journey for a life outside their home country is better than staying put. The Eritrean refugee crisis in Europe took a sharp upward turn in 2014, as the UNHCR numbers show. And tragedies, like the drowning of hundreds of Eritrean refugees off the Italian island of Lampedusa in October 2013, demonstrate the perils of the journey west and how desperate these people are.

Even when Eritrean refugees go no further than Sudan and Ethiopia, they face a grim situation. According to Lul Seyoum, director of International Centre for Eritrean Refugees and Asylum Seekers (ICERAS), Eritrean refugees in a number of camps inside Sudan and Ethiopia face trafficking, and other gross human rights violations. They are afraid to speak and meet with each other. She said, that though information is hard to get out, many Eritreans find themselves in tough situations in these isolated camps, and the situation has worsened since Sudan and Eritrea became closer politically.

Eritrea had a hostile relationship with Sudan during the 1990s. It supported the Sudan People's Liberation Movement, much to the anger of President Al Bashir who was locked in a bitter war with the people of now-independent South Sudan. Today tensions have eased considerably, and President Afwerki has much friendly relations with Sudan to the detriment of then tens of thousands of Eritrean refugees in Sudan.

A former Eritrean ministry of education official, who is a refugee now based in the UK and who does not want to be named because of safety fears, believes there's no freedom of expression for Eritreans in Ethopian camps, such as Shimelba.

The official says in 2013 a group of Eritrean refugees came together at a camp to express their views on the boat sinking near Lampedusa and they were abused by the Ethiopian authorities who then fired at them with live bullets.

Seyoum believes that the movement of Eritreans in camps in Ethiopia is restricted. "The Ethiopian government does not allow them to leave the camps without permission," she says. Even for those who get permission to leave very few end up in Ethiopia, instead through corrupt mechanisms are trafficked to Sudan. According to Human Rights Watch, hundreds of Eritreans have been enslaved in torture camps in Sudan and Egypt over the past 10 years, many enduring violence and rape at their hands of their traffickers in collusion with state authorities.

Even when Eritreans make it to the West, they are still afraid to speak publicly and many are fearful for their families back home. Now based in London, Debesai is a

TV presenter at Sports News Africa. As an exile who has taken a stance against the regime of President Afewerki, he has faced harassment and threats. He is harassed over social media, on Twitter and Facebook. Over coffee, he shows me a tweet he's just received from Tesfa News, a so-called "independent online magazine", in which they accuse him of being a "backstabber" against the government and people of Eritrea. Others face

There are no opposition parties and no independent media. No independent public gatherings or civil society organisations are permitted

similar threats, including the former education ministry official.

For this piece, a number of Eritreans said they did not want to be interviewed because they were afraid of the consequences. But Debesai said: "It takes time to overcome the past, so that even for those in exile in the West the imprisonment continues." He adds: "These refugees come out of a physical prison and go into psychological imprisonment." ⊠

© Ismail Einashe
www.indexoncensorship.org

Ismail Einashe is a journalist and a researcher, based in London. He tweets @IsmailEinashe

A very human picture

44(1): 50/52 | DOI: 10.1177/0306422015570526

Award-winning reportage illustrator **Olivier Kugler** talks about working in Iraq's Domiz refugee camp and how he draws the stories he hears

I VISITED THE Domiz refugee camp in Iraqi Kurdistan to document the stories of the people there through my illustrations, including the one of Ahmed (see right). At the beginning of December 2013, I spent two weeks in conversations with refugees I met on long walks through the camp. I conducted about 30 interviews, and took countless photographs.

Most of the interviews were done in tents and small houses where refugees live, and most of the interviewees were men. I was accompanied by a translator and a public awareness officer from Médecins Sans Frontières.

Carpets were laid on concrete floors or sometimes even bare soil. There were no chairs, or tables and they cooked using basic gas stoves. It was cold outside, but warm tea was always offered. Some interviews were carried out in hairdressers, or mobile phone and TV repair shops. We had an interview in a bakery and others in restaurants.

I asked refugees why they had left Syria and how they had managed to get out, I asked about their experiences as refugees and what they thought the future held.

Most of the young men I interviewed left Syria because they did not want to get drafted into the military, some of them had also fled from active duty. Many people, especially from the Kurdish regions of Syria in the north-east, left because the economic situation had become so bad. There were no jobs. Food and fuel prices were high, and there were frequent power cuts. Aside from this there were, of course, the people who used to live in cities like Damascus, Aleppo, and Homs, who were forced to flee because of the fighting.

At the beginning of each conversation I asked the translator to inform the interviewees that I was an illustrator creating a series of drawings documenting refugees' circumstances and that the drawings and interviews might get published internationally. Some of those I met were reluctant to be interviewed and photographed, as they were afraid that if they spoke out either they or their relatives could get into trouble with one of the warring parties back in Syria. However, they were okay as long as I focused on their experiences in the camp, and not what happened in Syria. On the other hand, there were many men who were not afraid they might appear in the media. They told me about their criticisms of the Syrian regime, the Free Syrian Army, or the jihadis.

Interviewing women was more difficult because of their culture, and those I did interview were connected to MSF. One interview was conducted in the organisation's mental health department, in the presence of a young Iraqi Kurdish psychotherapist. The patient was a young mother, whose husband was arrested by the police two years ago. She told me that she hadn't heard anything from him since, and has lost all hope of ever →

→ seeing him again. She cried as she told me that her children always get sad when they see other children playing with their fathers. "It breaks my heart," she said.

Sometimes the interviews were difficult to conduct as the translator's English was not very good. I will also admit that my knowledge of the situation in Syria was a bit patchy at the beginning. I often had to repeat questions and ask for more explanations and found the encounters difficult on an emotional level. I was very aware of my privileged position, holding a German passport and a ticket for a return flight. The interviewees on the other hand were in a desperate situation with little hope of improving their circumstances in the near future. I was often approached and asked for advice by those wanting to leave for England or Germany.

When I returned to London, I began to look again at the photographs I had taken and wanted to draw most of them, starting to work on small sketches, based on the images. I then started to work on the larger pencil drawings, which were then scanned and coloured digitally. While working, I often listened to recordings of the interviews. It is very important for me to have met the people I draw. I work best if I have a connection with those I am depicting. ☒

© Olivier Kugler
www.indexoncensorship.org

Olivier Kugler's reportage illustrations were exhibited at the Fumetto International Comix Festival in Lucerne, Switzerland, in 2014. He was winner of the V&A Illustration Award in 2011

In limbo in world's oldest refugee camps

44(1): 53/56 | DOI: 10.1177/0306422015569438

Novelist **Tim Finch** looks at the growing problem of long-term refugee camps housing 10 million people, which have morphed into makeshift towns, and where undocumented residents can be trapped for decades

THERE ARE MANY instances in our world where a vast human tragedy lurks beneath a set of bland initials. Such is the case with PRS. It stands for Protracted Refugee Situations, the official definition of a situation where 25,000 or more refugees from the same country have taken refuge in another country for five years or more.

Given the misery such limbo inflicts, it would be good to report that it is a relatively rare occurrence. Sadly it isn't. The UN reckons there are around 15.5 million refugees in the world today – and by some estimates around two-thirds of them are in protracted refugee situations. The largest current refugee crisis – the displacement of more than three million Syrians into Jordan, Lebanon, Turkey and Iraq – has not been going on long enough to count as a PRS, though many experts think it is only a matter of time.

It is the immediate refugee crises like that in Syria or, closer to home, people trying to get across the Mediterranean in overloaded boats that tend to dominate the headlines. But the bigger, though less told, story is of refugees languishing in refugee camps, normally just over the border from their home country, for years and years and years.

It's difficult to be precise about which is the world's oldest refugee camp. As time

passes, temporary camps can take on a permanence that makes them almost indistinguishable from other towns or from city suburbs. However, one of the oldest camps is surely Cooper's Camp in West Bengal, India. It dates from the time of partition in 1947 when a large number of Hindus living in mainly Muslim East Bengal (now Bangladesh) fled across the border. Nearly 70 years on, Cooper's Camp is still home to some 7,000 people.

It no longer resembles a camp. There is no boundary fence, and there are no guards or refugee agency buildings. In fact, Cooper's Camp looks like a typical Indian village. Its many problems – inadequate housing, lack of infrastructure, general poverty, high unemployment, low educational attainment and poor physical and mental health – are common enough. What marks it out from all the other miserable towns and villages in the sub-continent is the status of its residents. Around 20 per cent of them, including some survivors from the 1947 exodus, still have not been given papers conferring Indian citizenship. This means they lack deeds to their land and don't have voting or other rights. Leaving the camp puts them at risk of deportation as illegal immigrants. They are effectively trapped in the camp, which, →

ABOVE: A man stands outside a shop in Kenya's Kakuma refugee camp, which has been in existence for over 20 years

though remote in some ways, is only 100 miles from the city of Kolkata.

Other refugees from partition who made it to Kolkata itself have fared better. Although they've had to go through legalisation processes which have sometimes stretched over decades, refugees living in areas of the city set aside for resettlement by the ministry of rehabilitation in 1947 have rebuilt their lives and transformed those areas. They are now considered to be normal residents of well-to-do, middle-class neighbourhoods.

However, being housed close to urban areas doesn't always result in refugees effectively being absorbed into the local population. Palestinian refugees on the West Bank have also been living in camps since the late 1940s. There are 750,000 of them registered by UNWRA – the specialist agency for Palestinian refugees – and they are scattered across 19 camps and other settlements. One camp – Shu'fat – actually lies within the municipal boundaries of Jerusalem. The refugees who live there are officially residents of the city and have access to some of Israel's social services, including healthcare. Their homes are also linked to the mains water and electricity supply.

But Shu'fat is by no means a suburb of Jerusalem. Access in and out is through military checkpoints and Shu'fat is hemmed in by Jewish settlements, an army base and Israel's notorious security wall. There are children living in Shu'fat who, like their parents and grandparents before them, have known no other life than this severely constricted existence – living inside the boundaries of the city and yet cut off from it, part of a relatively prosperous conurbation yet still reliant on the UN for many of the basics of life.

In contrast to many of the Palestinian camps, the world's largest concentration of refugee camps, in the Dadaab area of eastern Kenya, does conform to the popular stereotype. Tens of thousands of tents and other basic shelters are laid out in grids in a desolate landscape of red earth and dry scrub, miles from major urban centres. This complex of camps has been in existence for more than 20 years and at its peak housed around 500,000 refugees, mainly from Somalia. There are signs that Dadaab might not follow the example of Cooper's Camp and Shu'fat and become, in effect, a permanent settlement. A tripartite agreement between the UN, Kenya and Somalia signed in 2013 has helped to facilitate the return and reintegration of up to 100,000 long-term inhabitants. On the other hand, the Kakuma camp complex in north-west Kenya, which has also been in existence for more than 20 years, has seen more refugees, mainly from South Sudan, arrive in recent years.

We cannot speak out and we have to be patient and passive. If we speak out too much, the chains tighten

Kakuma is perhaps best known in the West because it was the home for many years of Valentino Achak Deng, one of Sudan's "Lost Boys" whose real-life story was turned into a novel – What is the What – by the US writer Dave Eggers. Before Valentino, who is writing for this magazine on how refugees are often not heard (See Lost boy found, Volume 44, 1/2015), got to Kakuma we learn in the novel of his experiences in a refugee camp in Ethiopia and how it was used as a recruiting ground for child soldiers by the SPLA rebel movement. Although international bodies are nominally in charge of most of the larger and longer-running refugee camps the real power inside the camps often lies with unofficial groups, sometimes of a terrorist or criminal nature. Once the camps become established, trading begins and small shops and service industries are set up. But because of the precarious governance and security in many camps, these →

→ enterprises are often subject to the extraction of extortionate rents by protection rackets. Drug-running, brothels and even paedophile rings are common, as are rapes. After dark, refugee camps can be as dangerous as any deprived inner city area, with the added disadvantage that it is not clear who "the authorities" are that should be providing protection. Sometimes the supposed "guards" are themselves complicit or active in violence – particularly against refugee women.

A major survey carried out in Dadaab found that many refugees felt their lives were hampered by a lack of information and by poor communication from administering agencies. While freedom of expression is

Around 20 per cent of them, including some survivors from the 1947 exodus, still have not been given papers conferring Indian citizenship

generally not actively suppressed in refugee camps – Kakuma, for instance, has its own independent news magazine, Kanere – refugees usually lack a voice in the way the camps are run, and speaking out against official or unofficial corruption and violence is risky. Another protracted refugee situation persists along the Thai/Burmese border where some 120,000 Burmese refugees languish in a string of camps. Conditions are poor, and abuses by the Thai army and police are common. Yet residents fear to complain. A Human Rights Watch report in 2012 quoted a resident as saying: "We are on Thai land so we have to be submissive. We cannot speak out and we have to be patient and passive. If we speak out too much, the chains tighten."

On the other hand, as Valentino Achak Deng's story showed, life in the camps can take on a semblance of normality over time. In the book, life in Kakuma after initial hardship becomes more comfortable: Deng goes to school, takes part in youth projects, plays in basketball teams and hangs out with his girlfriend. All the same, Deng's goal always remained to escape from the camps and start a new life in the world outside. In the end Deng was resettled in the United States. For most refugees, however, such a prospect is vanishingly small. UNHCR estimates that nearly one million refugees globally are in need of resettlement (including Syrians). But the number of places provided by the world's governments is only around 80,000 a year. So for most of the men, women and children living in PRS, their life in limbo is likely to stretch well into the future.

As yet the Kilis camp in Turkey has only been in existence for a couple of years and its excellent facilities have earned it the sobriquet: the "five-star refugee camp". But for all the well-equipped mobile homes, with their televisions and solar panels, for all the Western-style supermarkets and public "plazas", for all the gleaming and efficient schools and medical centres, none of the residents sees a long-term future in this soulless, artificial settlement. As one man told The New York Times when one reporter visited Kilis in early 2014: "It's hard for us. Inside we're unhappy. In my heart, it's temporary, not permanent." He says that and we feel his anguish. But in 10 or even 20 years time, it is highly possible that he'll still be there: trapped, like so many other millions, in a PRS. ☒

© Tim Finch
www.indexoncensorship.org

Tim Finch is a broadcaster, working for the BBC for many years. He is a former director of communications for the British Refugee Council. His novel The House of Journalists (Vintage), is just been published in paperback. He tweets @TimAAFinch

Sound and fury

44(1): 57/59 | DOI: 10.1177/0306422015571885

Heaven 17's **Martyn Ware** talks with **Rachael Jolley** about creating the soundscape for London's #WithSyria vigil, to try and tell stories from the enormous Zaatari refugee camp in Jordan, and his involvement in a music project in Zimbabwe

MUSICIAN MARTYN WARE is still touring with 80s synthpop band Heaven 17, but his new passion is soundscapes: sound installations in public spaces allowing people to walk through different recordings, creating a documentary collage of sound. One of the most powerful of these formed part of the #WithSyria event held in London's Trafalgar Square last year, to focus attention on the impact of three years of war in Syria. Ware and his partners from Illustrious, the company Ware co-founded, collected and recorded stories from people living in the massive Zaatari camp in Jordan, where currently, according to the UNHCR around 84,000 mostly Syrian refugees are living. They worked closely with international charities Save the Children, Amnesty International and Oxfam, who were organising the whole event. It had impact; it is estimated that 375 million people were tweeting, reading about and watching the event.

Those standing in the square heard recordings of refugees speaking about their own experiences, in English and Arabic, as well as children singing. Its power, as I remember standing there, was that there was no moving video to distract attention, so you stood and listened to the voices.

Ware said of the recordings: "All of the speech, everything, came from people within the camp. No actors did anything, it was all real. And a lot of it was quite desperate."

But they also wanted to get over the normal of day-to-day life and some of the hope for the future: "So looking at the Zaatari camp and the privation they have to suffer, we heard stories of what people are doing there to make it a tolerable environment. Like renaming some of the streets, the Champs-Élysées, for instance – a street which is literally just a dirt path through the middle of a bunch of tents – and building their own private exchange-based economy within the camp."

The #WithSyria project was held to recognise the three-year anniversary of the beginning of the crisis in Syria, and to try make more people around the world aware of the conditions, the massive displacement of people, and the impact of the war.

"We had a huge number of recordings. We gathered a lot of sounds from local musicians living in the camp. A lot of people who were displaced from Libya were very affluent – this isn't just poor people who are starving and the third-world cliché in general – it's not a third world issue at all really, this is more to do with displacement. So a lot of them had their own instruments, a lot of them had recording devices, although electricity is a problem, of course."

ABOVE: A girl releases a #WithSyria balloon in Zaatari refugee camp, Jordan

→ There's a lot of misery there as well, not to sugar-coat it; it's a horrible environment and the adults, especially, just want to go home."

He thinks the kind of soundscape he creates works in a different way to news reporting on the camp. "There have been some very good pieces of journalism written about it but it's not appealing from a news point of view- it's on a grand, epic scale that people can't comprehend."

While doing research, those making recordings found former professional musicians living in the camp, and wanted to use

Its power was that there was no moving video to distract attention, so you stood and listened to the voices

their skills too. "What was really fascinating and inspiring was the songs they were writing directly related to their experience there, and when we played some of those back as part of the soundscape in Trafalgar Square there were refugees there who were crying. The sound of the instruments obviously typical of that region were obviously very emotive for them, and then there's the really realistic sounding children singing in their classroom, singing beautiful songs, which we placed in one corner of Trafalgar

Square, making it sound as if they were really there."

Ware, who says he is hoping there is a chance to do a follow-up piece from Zaatari, is also working to set up a music project of a different kind in Zimbabwe, along with an organisation called Agencia. He also works with Manchester University's In Place of War project which researches and develops music in countries with armed conflict. "We are collecting musicians, musical instruments and recording devices, and working with these townships just outside of Makokoba, near Bulawayo. They've got 95 per cent unemployment in the area, and Zimbabwe used to be quite a rich country. They've got nothing to do, they're bored, so a lot of the time they're drinking and there's also nothing for the kids to do. So we're building a creative hub, and raising money for it, together with the local parent group. We're shipping out container loads of stuff for Harare as well."

One of the ideas is to create a global network of musicians, exchanging ideas. In Zimbabwe, they have already made an album with some singers they met. "Some of them were just teenagers who rapped and did hip hop, some were poets and some more traditional musicians like drummers. And in three days, without any preparation at all, we made an album with them. We are working on it now, fine-tuning it and mixing it together. A friend of mine, a British musician based in Manchester called Aniff Akinola (from Backyard Dog), Rodney P (who started out with London Posse) and another artist called Fallacy, were all out there working with them, and doing collaborations, with the idea to raise money for Makokoba so we can get this creative hub off the ground."

Ware sees music and sound recordings as powerful both as a creative outlet for Syrians and Zimbabwean townships, and as a different experience for audiences hearing them. Both projects give people a direct

ABOVE: Banksy artwork of a Syrian girl with a balloon was projected on to Nelson's Column at the Stand #WithSyria rally, Trafalgar Square, London to mark the third anniversary of the crisis in Syria, March 2014

voice (literally in the case of the #WithSyria vigil) to the world they might not otherwise have. ☒

© Rachael Jolley
www.indexoncensorship.org

Rachael Jolley is editor of Index on Censorship. Follow the magazine on @index_magazine

Sheltering against resentment

44(1): 60/63 | DOI: 10.1177/0306422015571517

When a wave of attacks on African migrants ripped through South Africa seven years ago, a church became a sanctuary for people who feared opening their mouths in public because they would give away their origins. Now its days as a refuge are over, but, as **Natasha Joseph** reports, xenophobia hasn't ended here

AS THE WORLD eased into party mode on 31 December last year, a few hundred people in a filthy church building in central Johannesburg weren't preparing to welcome 2015: they were packing up their meagre belongings and trying to find a new home.

They were the last of the almost 35,000, mostly Zimbabwean, immigrants who sought refuge in the Central Methodist Church in South Africa's city of gold. Seven years ago, it became a safe haven for people seeking protection from violent xenophobic attacks that were ripping through the country. South Africa is far more economically stable than its neighbours in the Southern African Development Community, and has long attracted hundreds of thousands of people seeking work and political security. Festering feelings that foreigners were stealing jobs, fuelling inequality and causing crime suddenly burst up and exploded. Riots broke out. Immigrants' businesses were torched. Anyone with a foreign accent feared being attacked in the street. In the most horrific case, Ernesto Alfabeto Nhamuave, a 35-year-old from Mozambique who was

working in Ramaphosa, a township in east Johannesburg, was set on fire in the street; the picture of him engulfed in flames, on his hands and knees as uniformed police officers looks on, went around the world.

In just two weeks, 62 people died and thousands were left homeless. It was particularly dangerous to be a foreigner moving around major cities like Johannesburg. Language, in particular the use of certain colloquialisms, made people targets. The Mail & Guardian newspaper reported that "as attacks on foreigners intensified and spread across Johannesburg, mobs began pulling people out of shopping queues and forcing them to take 'tests' to establish their nationality".

While this was going on, George, a Malawian man who tended my parents' garden every weekend took time off from his various jobs and returned to Malawi – because, he told me then, he was frightened to be stopped on public transport and ordered to speak isiXhosa, the most commonly spoken African language in the Western Cape province. He had heard of people ("people like me" he said), being thrown from moving

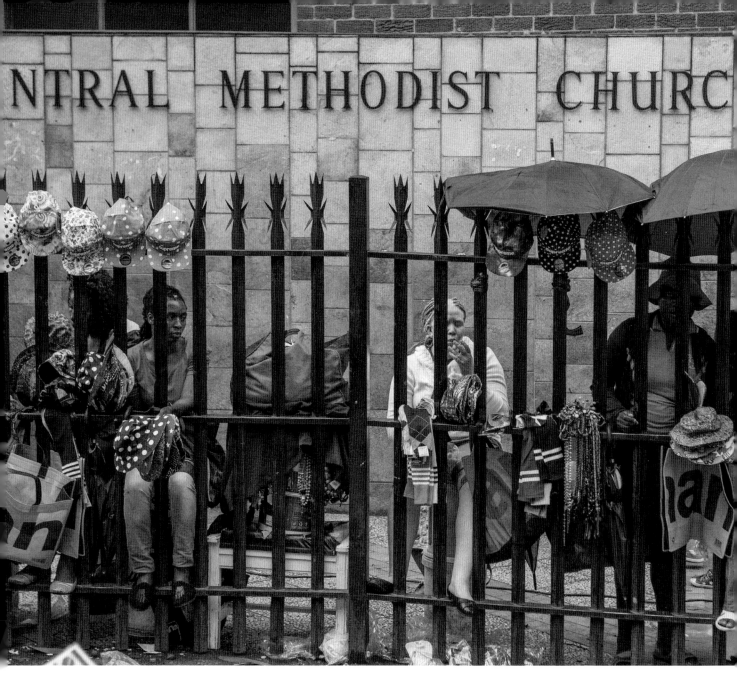

ABOVE: The Central Methodist Church, Johannesburg, was a safe haven for immigrants for seven years before its role as a shelter came to an end in December 2014. Pictured are some of the 35,000 people who have sought refuge in that time

trains because they could not identify body parts or use simple words in isiXhosa. Rather than risk his life, George stayed silent and spent a few months unemployed in Malawi before returning to resume his life in South Africa.

Many immigrants were not so lucky, and places like the Central Methodist Church offered at least some protection by opening its doors to terrified immigrants. But the building was never meant to be a long-term home. Like many buildings in Johannesburg's city centre, which are overcrowded and ill-maintained, it degenerated into a slum as more and more people came. A reporter from the

South African Sunday Times who visited the Central Methodist Church in December 2014, described filth, debris, broken lifts and people sleeping in stairwells.

By then, the church's superintendent Bishop Paul Verryn, 62, was at the tail-end of a long battle that had seen him repeatedly butt heads with church leaders from South Africa's Methodist church. In 2010, it suspended him, complaining he had taken decisions about the church building and its occupants without authority. The bishop's suspension was quickly lifted, but for the next four years he fought to make the Central Methodist Church as good a temporary home as he →

→ could. By the end of 2014, though, it was clear that the church could no longer serve as a safe shelter. Verryn was moved to a new position and, on December 31, the remaining residents' time ran out.

Verryn spoke to Index on Censorship on that last day, just after he had delivered his last sermon there. He said the church had been a shelter even before 2008, for those who were "quite seriously broken from the trauma of leaving their country and making the trip to South Africa". They came from

He had heard of people being thrown from moving trains because they could not use simple words in isiXhosa

countries racked by decades of civil war, political and economic unrest: the Democratic Republic of the Congo, Somalia and Zimbabwe.

Verryn said that "for the longest time there were about 50 people in the building". But, in 2008, "there was an explosion of people moving into the building after the xenophobic attacks – about 1,500 moved in". Some Verryn even accommodated at his own home in Soweto. Many of these people, he recalls, were suffering a double trauma: they had fled violence, or even war, in their own countries and, after building new lives for themselves, were thrown back into a kind of hell by the neighbours they'd trusted in South Africa. One man who lived with Verryn for a time was so severely distressed that when he slept any loud noise would trigger flashbacks and memories of torture.

During the church's seven years as home and haven, Verryn preached to his congregation about the plight of those seeking shelter. In his sermons, he tried to educate South Africans about welcoming people from around the continent and world into their backyard,

and many donated food and clothes to the foreigners living in the church.

By the end of 2014, even Verryn knew it was time to close the church's doors. Central Methodist Church wasn't meant to be a "destination", he told Index on Censorship – rather, it was a stop on the journey that he hoped would see many people reintegrated into their South African neighbourhoods. "Though we provide a little bit of shelter from the street, this is not the ideal place, where people will be sleeping on the steps with no privacy for years."

Attacks against foreigners remain uncomfortably common. The South African government insists that what victims and the media describe as xenophobia is actually just garden-variety crime. A cabinet statement from May 2013 read: "The cabinet is cautious not to label this violence as xenophobia because preliminary evidence indicates that these acts may be driven primarily by criminality." But a trawl of South African newspapers reveals at least two or three reported attacks on foreign-owned shops each month, and as victims often complain that they are frightened of the police, it's likely that the problem is vastly underreported.

South Africa holds its local government elections in 2016, and jobs, education and the provision of housing and sanitation will be top of people's minds. Competition for jobs (South Africa's unemployment rate was above 25 per cent in the third quarter of 2014) is fierce and foreigners are seen as "stealing" jobs from locals, whether by entering the formal labour market or setting up their own businesses. In 2013, the Gauteng Greater Business Forum denied that its members were actively organising xenophobic attacks on foreign-owned grocery shops – but went on to say that foreign-owned shops were bad for the economy and people from elsewhere in Africa and from Asian countries, such as Bangladesh and Pakistan, who most commonly run their own businesses, should be placed in refugee camps.

Central Methodist Church may have closed its doors, but feelings, nationwide, still run deep. Immigrants may not be stopped in the street and ordered to answer questions in Zulu or isiXhosa to prove that they 'belong', but judgements persist. "We are never not vulnerable, especially as a country that has been struggling with a propensity to be prejudiced all the time," said Verryn. "You don't come out of a history of centuries of oppression and think that all of us in this country are not susceptible to making irrational decisions based on tribe or gender. We have a long way to go, particularly in a nation where the disparity between haves and have-nots is this great." ▨

© Natasha Joseph
www.indexoncensorship.org

Additional reporting by Athandiwe Saba

Natasha Joseph is news editor at City Press, Johannesburg, and a contributing editor to Index on Censorship magazine

Understanding how language matters

44(1): 64/66 | DOI: 10.1177/0306422015571292

Writer **Kao Kalia Yang** on how her Hmong family struggled to fit in, first in a Thai refugee camp, and later as US immigrants

KUV HLUB KOJ. The words mean "I love you". A hand on the forehead, the gentle push of hair from a fevered face. The gesture means "I love you".

Movement in the mouth of an adult. Hungry, we, the little ones, reached for their mouths. A small moment. A piece of chewed meat, the soft bits of rice, proffered in bare hands. The actions mean, "I love you".

I was born into the Hmong language. I knew that there were many ways of communicating love. I understood from an early age that I was fortunate to be born to a people so plentiful in the gentle observations of care and devotion. And yet, growing up in Ban Vinai refugee camp in Thailand and then later in the USA as refugees of war, too often I felt far too keenly the things we lacked, the languages we didn't know, the places we couldn't belong.

Thai was an imperative language in Thailand. While most of the adults in my life understood and could communicate in Lao, few of them could move fluently in Thai. Still, they understood the commands and could respond slowly to the questions asked of them. The older cousins learned Thai in school. They could do simple arithmetic and argue in the language if they were so moved. I didn't go to school. I was just a kid with an uneven fringe, a little girl with bruised legs and dark, round eyes. All I knew was

that a person had to know some Thai to buy food from the vendors that visited the camp during the day, or enter the one-baht movie houses that sat high on the hills surrounding the camp. I didn't know any Thai, thus I could not move freely in Thailand – never mind that there were Thai men with guns stationed at the roads holding all the Hmong people inside, regardless of whether they spoke Thai well or not.

In Saint Paul, Minnesota we, my older sister and I, were tested in English. All I knew was A, B and C. My older sister knew that every colour was yellow and that there was an "s" behind every English word. We were placed in the same classroom. I was in first grade. She was in third grade.

Outside in the playground, I was bouncing a ball. A boy approached me. He said some words I couldn't understand. He wanted my ball but I still wanted to play with it. He tried to take it. I tried to take it back. My older sister, who had polio as a child in the camps and walked with a limp, flew from somewhere and tackled him to the ground. Her little feet planted on either side of his body, she yelled at him in Hmong, "*Txhob ua li ko rau kuv tus viv ncaus.*" In our language, it was love. She was saying, "Don't do that to my sister", but our language did not translate into English. The teachers pulled us all apart.

My sister and I were expelled from the school.

We sat in front of our black-and-white television set watching Tom and Jerry. Tom and Jerry didn't speak much of any language. They played tricks on each other. Tom tried to eat Jerry. We laughed and laughed. Our hands covered our faces. In a life where we didn't get to play many games, we felt we understood their game.

At work, beside tall machines, our father and mother scrambled to keep up with the assembly line. The parts were heavy. The pieces were small. They squinted and they worked fast with their hands. When the seasons passed and the years grew long, when the snow fell outside and melted away again, when the crocus came out with their bright blue blooms and the crab apples unleashed their fluffy, flowery fire, my mother and father's hands lost their speed and their ears, beside the loud machines, stopped working so well. The supervisors yelled at them in English, "Not fast enough. No good." The shaking of their heads sent their words home.

Around our little table with the uneven stand, Dawb and I watched as our mother and father put their heads in their hands. We saw their hands tremble although we did not hear them cry. They said, "How we are going to survive in this life? We don't even know the language."

Years later, when the language was no longer new and scary, Dawb and I sat around a different table, our heads in our hands, saying to each other, "How are we going to make this work?" Our mother and father no longer worked. Their hands were crippled by carpal tunnel syndrome, where vibrations had numbed their nerve endings, and even far from the loud machines they could not get away from its cries, the sounds of pistons and metal clashing resounded in their ears.

I was a teacher of English. I taught young people how to read and write in the language.

ABOVE: Kao Kalia Yang (left) with her family in Thailand. The family lived in the Ban Vinai refugee camp in the north-east of Thailand for over six years after fleeing Laos during the Vietnam War

I was a writer in English, a language that continued to play tricks on my tongue – the way Tom and Jerry played it, like a game that would continue forever, the hunger and the chase, the tricks of the trade. I wasn't making enough to support two families, my parent's and my own small one. The same was true of Dawb. But neither of us would say so in any language on Earth. Instead, we said, "We'll find a way." I wrote in my journal, "There have been times when I've feared that life had nothing more to give. There have been times when I've feared I've had nothing more to offer. Each time, I was wrong."

In Hmong, we hear many things from our parents. My mother says that we don't cry because of poverty. She says that she's lived her whole life poor and that if she was going →

Credit: Coffee House Press

ABOVE: Writer Kao Kalia Yang grew up in Ban Vinai refugee camp in Thailand

→ to cry because she was poor, she would have to cry every single day. My father says that our lives may be poor but our hearts are not. He says that he would rather live with a rich heart in high poverty than live in great wealth and hold a meager heart safe. Together, their words give us a blanket against the cold winter of despair, but in English, all we hear from them, in the world we live in is, "Hello, I'm fine. Thank you" or worse, "I'm sorry".

The man at the gas station was angry because my father and I were holding up the line. My father's chapped hands dropped the coins the teller had given us. Together, my father and I were on the ground, picking up the coins. The man stood with his feet planted far apart. He wore brown working boots. He tapped his right foot impatiently. My father and I both tried to move faster in our efforts. When we picked up the last coin, we both stood up. The man looked down at my father from his great height, down the length of a straight nose. He said, "You people are doing nothing but slowing us down in this country. You have given us nothing but trouble."

My father said, "I'm sorry." My heart was ready to say many things, but the words did not come to me. They were stuck in my throat – rocks of meaning I could not sculpt fast enough to communicate my love for my father, for my people, for me, and the life we have lived – trapped in spaces in search of belonging. ⊠

© Kao Kalia Yang
www.indexoncensorship.org

Kao Kalia Yang is a Hmong American writer and author of The Latehomecomer: A Hmong Family Memoir. She has also wrote The Place Where We Were Born, a documentary about experiences of Hmong refugees in the USA

Global view

44(1): 67/68 | DOI: 10.1177/0306422015570808

Jodie Ginsberg criticises increasing limitations on students' access to controversial debates or books at US and UK universities

SOMETHING IS GOING wrong at universities. Institutions that should be crucibles for new thinking, at the forefront of challenges to established thought and practice, are instead actively shutting down debate, and shying away from intellectual confrontation.

Driven by the notion that students should not be exposed to ideas they find – or might find – offensive or troubling, student groups and authorities are increasingly squeezing out free speech – by banning controversial speakers, denying individuals or groups platforms to speak, and eliminating the possibility of "accidental" exposure to new ideas through devices such as trigger warnings.

The trend was particularly noticeable last year when a number of invited speakers withdrew from university engagements – or had their invitations rescinded – following protests from students and faculty members. Former US Secretary of State Condoleezza Rice withdrew from a planned address at Rutgers University in New Jersey after opposition from those who cited her involvement in the Iraq war and the Bush administration's torture of terrorism suspects; Brandeis University in Massachusetts cancelled plans to award an honorary degree to Islam critic Ayaan Hirsi Ali; and Christine Lagarde backed out of a speech at Smith College following objections by students over the acts of the International Monetary Fund, which Lagarde runs. In the UK, the University of East London banned an Islamic preacher for his views on homosexuality. And a new law – a counter-terrorism bill – was proposed in Britain that could be used to force universities to ban speakers considered "extremist".

Registering your objection to something or someone is one thing. Indeed, the ability to do that is fundamental to free expression. Actively seeking to prevent that person from speaking or being heard is quite another. It is a trend increasingly visible in social media – and its appearance within universities is deeply troubling.

It is seen not just in the way invited speakers are treated, but it stretches to the academic fraternity itself. Last year, the University of Illinois at Urbana-Champaign withdrew a job offer to academic Steven Salaita following critical posts he made on Twitter about Israel.

In an open letter, Phyllis Wise, University of Illinois at Urbana-Champaign chancellor, in an open letter, wrote: "A pre-eminent university must always be a home for difficult discussions and for the teaching of diverse ideas... What we cannot and will not tolerate at the University of Illinois are personal and disrespectful words or actions that demean and abuse either viewpoints themselves →

→ or those who express them. We have a particular duty to our students to ensure that they live in a community of scholarship that challenges their assumptions about the world but that also respects their rights as individuals."

These incidents matter because, as education lecturer Joanna Williams wrote in The Telegraph newspaper: "If academic freedom is to be in anyway meaningful it must be about far more than the liberty to be surrounded by an inoffensive and bland con-

Views that make us feel uncomfortable are fundamental to a free society

sensus. Suppressing rather than confronting controversial arguments prevents criticality and the advance of knowledge, surely the antithesis of what a university should be about?"

Yet, increasingly, universities seem to want to shut down controversy, sheltering behind the dangerous notion that protecting people from anything but the blandest and least contentious ideas is the means to keep them "safe", rather than encouraging students to have a wide base of knowledge. In the US, some universities are considering advising students that they don't have to read material they they may find upsetting, and if they don't their course mark would not suffer, according to the Los Angeles Times.

In the UK, increasing intolerance for free expression is manifest in the "no platform" movement – which no longer targets speakers or groups that incite violence against others, but a whole host of individuals and organisations that other groups simply find distasteful, or in some way disqualified from speaking on other grounds.

The decision to cancel an abortion debate at Oxford in late 2014, which would have been held between two men – and

noted free speech advocates – came after a slew of objections, including a statement from the students' union that decried the organisers for having the temerity to invite people without uteruses to discuss the issue.

Encountering views that make us feel uncomfortable, that challenge our worldview are fundamental to a free society. Universities are places where that encounter should be encouraged and celebrated. They should not be places where ideas are wrapped in cotton wool, where academic freedom comes to mean having a single kind of approved thinking, or where only certain "approved" individuals are allowed to speak on a given topic.

Index on Censorship knows well the importance of the scholar in freedom of expression. Though we have come to be known as Index, the charity itself is officially called Writers and Scholars International, an effort to capture as simply as possible the individuals whom we intended to support from the outset. The title was never intended to be exclusive, but the inclusion of "scholar" signals the importance our founders attached to the role of the academic as a defender and promoter of free speech. In 2015, as we watch the spaces for free expression narrow, we will work doubly hard to ensure that university remains an arena for the clash of ideas, not the closure of minds. X

© Jodie Ginsberg
www.indexoncensorship.org

Jodie Ginsberg is the CEO of Index on Censorship

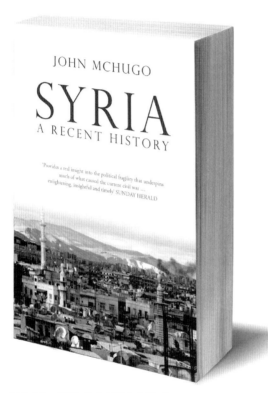
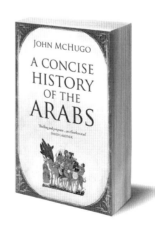

ABOVE: People place flowers representing victims of sexual violence in Nicaragua on the staircase of the Monument of the Angel of Independence during a protest in Mexico City, October 2011

IN FOCUS

In this section

Outbreaks under wraps

44(1): 72/75 | DOI: 10.1177/0306422015570534

Denial and lack of information about ebola caused hundreds of avoidable deaths in west Africa. From Spanish flu to Aids to Sars, cover-ups and misinformation have fuelled epidemics. **Alan Maryon-Davis** looks at what the world has, and hasn't, learnt from the past

OF ALL THE barriers faced by those battling ebola in west Africa, perhaps the most deadly was the web of denial that severely hampered efforts during the first several months of the outbreak. Wherever they went, health workers and relief organisations found that people were either reluctant to admit that anything serious was going on, or insisted that the numbers of victims were lower than they really were and the situation was fully under control. From remote villages to central government, this failure to accept the reality and urgency of what was unfolding led to frustrating delays and hundreds, perhaps thousands, of lives lost unnecessarily.

In July 2014, Médecins Sans Frontières, the NGO fighting desperately to keep a lid on the spread in Guinea and its next-door neighbours Sierra Leone and Liberia, openly criticised Guinean ministers for deliberately downplaying the extent of the outbreak. "They are very much annoyed by ebola, because of the investors," said one MSF official. "The government's first concern was not to scare outsiders. They wanted to minimise the cases."

Despite the repeated pleas from NGOs on the ground, and top experts such as Professor Peter Piot, director of the London School of Hygiene and Tropical Medicine,

who co-discovered the ebola virus in 1976 following an outbreak in what is now the Democratic Republic of the Congo, the World Health Organization and the international community were woefully slow to respond on anything like the scale needed. He told The Guardian in December: "It reminds me of the beginning of Aids. The same attitude prevailed. Just – no, it is not us, it does not exist. Precious time was wasted." Professor Piot added: "WHO was silent. Governments denied it. All that meant [was] that it got out of control."

Ebola and Aids are not the only examples of infectious diseases that have spread because the authorities denied how serious the outbreaks were. By far the most notorious and most devastating in terms of lives lost was the great Spanish flu pandemic of 1918, which killed at least 50 million people worldwide. In its early stages all news and information on the disease was censored by belligerent governments – a policy that greatly hindered attempts to prevent its spread and undoubtedly contributed to many thousands of avoidable deaths.

But Piot's comparison of the spread of ebola and Aids is chillingly apt. Acquired Immune Deficiency Syndrome first came to world attention in 1981 as cases of a strange and lethal form of pneumonia appeared

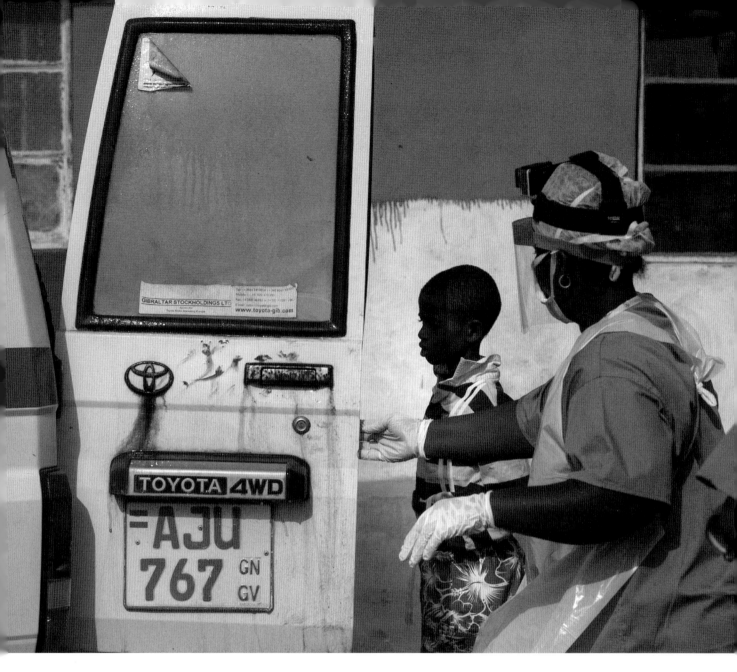

ABOVE: A health worker escorts nine-year-old Maraila, a suspected ebola victim, to an ambulance in Sierra Leone, December 2014

among gay men in New York and Francisco, and subsequently among intravenous drug users, people receiving blood transfusions and heterosexual couples. Soon it was found to be widespread across the world, and especially prevalent in sub-Saharan Africa.

In 1983 a virus was identified that was considered by international experts to be the causative agent for Aids and was dubbed Human Immunodeficiency Virus (HIV). Yet, despite this strong consensus, a sizeable and remarkably influential anti-HIV lobby emerged, largely from within the gay community in the USA, denying that the virus had any part to play in the disease.

Spearheaded by the renowned US molecular biologist Peter Duesberg, who asserted that HIV was simply a harmless "passenger" virus, the deniers did much to fuel the

There was a shroud of secrecy imposed by the Chinese government in the early stages of the Sars epidemic

notion that Aids was likely to be caused by some unknown environmental factor rather than unsafe sex. This belief was to have →

→ disastrous consequences for human health – particularly in South Africa where Aids was raging out of control.

In 2000, the South African government of President Thabo Mbeki enthusiastically embraced the idea that HIV was not to blame, that proven anti-retroviral therapy was ineffective, and that Aids was mainly linked to poverty. His then health minister, Manto Tshabalala-Msimang, focused on promoting good nutrition, particularly beetroot, garlic, potatoes, olive oil and lemon juice, as the best way to fend off the disease.

For years the South African government continued to drag its feet in rolling out a programme of anti-retroviral drug therapy for patients with advanced Aids and for HIV-positive pregnant women. This failing was described by British ex-Cabinet minister Peter,

As the current ebola crisis has made all too clear, secrecy and denial serve only to fuel potential catastrophe

now Lord, Mandelson as "genocide by sloth". In 2006 the United Nations special envoy for Aids in Africa, Stephen Lewis, accused ministers of promoting a "lunatic fringe" approach to HIV/Aids. He said the South African government had been "obtuse, dilatory, and negligent about rolling out treatment".

Finally in 2008, President Mbeki was ousted, together with his health minister. The incoming minister, Barbara Hogan, announced that "the era of denialism is over completely in South Africa". Tragically, this conversion came too late for the more than 330,000 Aids sufferers in South Africa who, according to researchers at Harvard University, died between 2000 and 2005. These people, the researchers say, might have been saved by timely anti-retroviral treatment.

While this shamefully misguided public health policy was playing out with disastrous consequences in South Africa, a different kind of "denialism" was occurring in southern China, which also threatened to endanger the entire world.

In late 2002 a farmer in Guangdong province fell ill with a high fever and sudden severe shortness of breath. He failed to respond to treatment with antibiotics and soon died of fulminating pneumonia and multiple organ failure, but not before further cases occurred among his family and other contacts. A doctor who had treated these patients checked in at the Metropole Hotel, Hong Kong, and fell suddenly ill himself, infecting several other hotel guests. Within a few weeks the outbreak of the deadly Sudden Acute Respiratory Syndrome (Sars) became a full-scale global health scare.

According to international agreements, an outbreak of this nature should immediately have been reported to the WHO, but for reasons unknown the Chinese authorities failed to do so until February 2003. By this time the epidemic was claiming dozens of lives every day and had started spreading to several other countries, notably Canada. The shroud of secrecy imposed by the Chinese government in the early stages of the epidemic undoubtedly hampered the international response and rendered other countries more vulnerable. Ultimately Sars infected over 8,000 people worldwide and killed a total of 774 before it was suppressed.

So, what lessons can be learned from these worrying examples of disease denial? Ten years after Sars, Margaret Chan, the director-general of WHO, insisted that important changes had been incorporated into international health regulations. Countries are now required to follow set procedures in preparing for, reporting on and responding to potential cross-border health threats, including complete openness in the provision of information.

"Because of the impetus coming from the Sars outbreak," Chan told The Canadian Press in 2013, "... all these requirements actually paved the way for countries to build their capacity and also understand the need for transparency."

But has greater transparency truly come about? Are countries, regions and cities around the world displaying the degree of openness needed to allow a timely and robust response to every potential international health threat?

The emergence of a new deadly Sars-like virus in Jeddah, Saudi Arabia, three years ago might suggest otherwise. Initially dubbed "camel flu", but afterwards officially named Middle East Respiratory Syndrome, the disease can cause sudden severe pneumonia with a 30 per cent fatality rate and has so far led to hundreds of cases throughout the Middle East and beyond. In Saudi Arabia alone more than 800 people have caught the disease. Many of those infected in the Arabian peninsula have had close contact with camels or camel products, but the virus can also pass from person to person through close contact of the sort experienced by family members and healthcare workers.

The Saudi government is currently working closely with WHO to monitor developments and find out more about the new virus, but this was not always so. In the early stages, according to news reports, international experts accused the health ministry of covertness and foot-dragging. Only since April 2014, when King Abdullah sacked the incumbent health minister, has reporting to the WHO, and the Saudi public at large, been more open.

We live in an increasingly globalised world. Every country depends on every other country for its health security. Viruses are constantly mutating and evolving. New infectious diseases can emerge anytime, anywhere. A single individual case can spark a global health emergency. As Anne Schuchat, director of the US National Center for Immunization and Respiratory Diseases, said in a press conference last May:

the next pandemic is "just a plane's ride away".

The ease with which pandemics can spread is the reason health systems around the world must be ready, willing and able to stamp out viral threats at the earliest opportunity. This means people at all levels must be informed, empowered and motivated to act promptly and decisively. As the current ebola crisis has made all too clear, secrecy and denial – whether by a village chief, health official or president – serve only to fuel potential catastrophe.

Has the vital importance of openness and transparency reached the people it needs to reach? Or will history repeat itself yet again? Let's hope the next pandemic doesn't prove to be one cover-up too many. ☒

© Alan Maryon-Davis
www.indexoncensorship.org

Alan Maryon-Davis is honorary professor in public health at King's College, London. He is past president of the UK's Faculty of Public Health and a former director of public health in Southwark, London

Trade secrets

44(1): 76/79 | DOI: 10.1177/0306422015569714

Drug-trafficking routes have changed, with Paraguay now playing an increasing role. As vicious gangs and corrupt officials try to gag reporters, **César Muñoz Acebes** looks at how one reporter's murder finally sparked a national debate

"I CALL THE REGIONAL office my regional jail," said reporter Cándido Figueredo, from ABC Color, one of Paraguay's leading newspapers. He is based in Pedro Juan Caballero, a border town and drug-trafficking hotspot. His office building is also his home, where he lives with his wife, under police protection. During his two decades reporting on local crime, his office and his car have been shot at four times. He has to travel 280 miles to the capital, Asunción, to feel safe to go out to a restaurant.

Paraguay's sparsely controlled 850-mile border with Brazil has been used for smuggling for decades, but Brazilian drug organisations have increased their operations here in recent years, according to police from both countries. In its last full survey of the region, in 2011, the United Nations Office on Drugs and Crime considered Paraguay the largest producer of marijuana in South America, accounting for 15 per cent of the world's harvest.

Paraguay is also turning from a transit country for cocaine trafficking to a producer country, according to its anti-drug agency, the Secretaría Nacional Antidrogas (SENAD), with the installation of laboratories in its territory financed by Brazilian gangs. As has been seen in other countries, the expansion of the drug networks is undermining institutions and leaving a trail of corruption, violent crime, and censorship.

The threat this poses to reporters and freedom of expression has never been clearer in Paraguay, a landlocked country a little bigger than Germany but with only 6.7 million people. Three journalists were killed there in 2014 – a record number. Santiago Ortiz, secretary-general of the Paraguayan Journalists Union (SPP), attributes the spike to the "freedom of action" that mafias enjoy in the country, because he believes they have infiltrated all branches of government. "We have to dismantle the narcostate that Paraguay has transformed into, or we will turn into Mexico," he told Index on Censorship.

The first death was in May 2014, when radio presenter Fausto Gabriel Alcaraz Garay was executed by two assailants in Pedro Juan Caballero. He worked for Radio Amambay, where he often denounced illegal activities. Senator Robert Acevedo, the radio station's owner, accused imprisoned drug traffickers of ordering the killing from jail. Radio reporter Edgar Pantaleón Fernández Fleitas was killed a month later in the northern city of Concepción, after returning from hosting his daily radio programme on Radio Belén Comunicaciones, on which he often accused judges, lawyers and prosecutors of corruption.

ABOVE: Journalist Pablo Medina at work in Paraguay's Mbaracayu Biological Reserve in 2014 before he was murdered later that year

But it was business as usual after those murders. The police did not make any arrests or name any suspects. Between 1991 and June 2014, 14 journalists had been killed in Paraguay, most of them because of their reports about drug trafficking, said Ortiz. Investigations led to convictions in only one case, according to the union.

Things changed after the third death in October. The victim, Pablo Medina, was a reporter in the town of Curuguaty for ABC Color, a newspaper owned by Aldo Zuccolillo, one of Paraguay's most influential men.

"The other two reporters were from regional radios. There was a bigger reaction in Pablo Medina's case, because all the media outlets felt attacked," said Rufo Medina (no relation), ABC Color's institutional relations manager.

Pablo Medina was gunned down by two assailants when he was driving home from

14 journalists have been killed, most because of their reports of drug trafficking

covering a story. Antonia Almada, one of two sisters travelling with him, was also killed, while her sister survived. President Horacio Cartes, who had not made any public statements after the death of the →

→ other two journalists, said Medina's and Almada's murders were "an attack against freedom of expression" in Paraguay.

Canindeyú, the province where Curuguaty is located, is one of the county's main areas for marijuana cultivation. Anti-drug officials roughly estimate Paraguay's annual production at between 30,000 and 45,000 tons, although they expect to have a more exact figure once they get results from a project that will use satellite images to detect plantations. Eighty per cent of Paraguayan marijuana ends up in Brazil, where its value increases almost fivefold.

Medina did not feel silenced by his brother's murder. But after his own death, other reporters might

Medina had received numerous threats over his work about illegal logging, drug trafficking and the alleged links between drug organisations and local politicians. According to ABC Color, some of those threats came from Vilmar Acosta, then mayor of Ypejhú (a municipality bordering Brazil), whom Medina had linked to drug-traffickers. The paper said that Acosta told Medina on the phone in 2010 that he would not allow anyone to "smear his name", and to be careful what wrote. The prosecutor's office has charged Acosta of ordering Medina's murder, which was supposedly carried out by Acosta's brother, Wilson, and their nephew, Flavio. All three are fugitives.

After the murder, the police searched a ranch owned by the Acosta family and found a marijuana-processing facility. They reported that it contained more than three tons of the drug at different stages of production.

In 2011 Vilmar Acosta had also been charged with homicide – along with his father, Vidal Acosta – and placed in pretrial detainee after human remains were found buried in the ranch. However, a tribunal released them less than a month later, and the case is still pending. Medina had alleged that Víctor Núñez, a member of the supreme court, had intervened to protect Acosta, an assertion that Núñez denied. Núñez resigned in December 2014 after the two main Paraguayan parties agreed to open proceedings in parliament for his dismissal.

Acosta's driver, Arnaldo Cabrera, told prosecutors that Acosta wanted to kill Medina for writing the articles that led to his arrest and for continuing to publish stories that damaged his interests. Medina also accused Acosta of ordering the killing in August 2014 of a political rival, former Ypejhú mayor Julián Núñez Benítez. Prosecutors charged him with that killing as well after Cabrera's testimony.

Many areas areas of the countryside in Paraguay are controlled by a handful of families, like the Acostas, who own huge tracts of land and have far-reaching influence on political and economic life. Ortiz says local police and prosecutors do not typically pursue investigations if the evidence points to influential figures.

After Medina's death, ABC Color turned its attention to politicians who had supported Acosta within his party, the Partido Colorado, especially Cristina Villalba, a member of the chamber of deputies. In a remarkable session in November 2014, the Senate made public confidential information from SENAD, which offered evidence of supposed links of three Partido Colorado congressmen and three other politicians to drug trafficking. As a result, congress set up a commission made up of senators and representatives to investigate Medina's death and the possible infiltration of public institutions by drug organisations.

In the meantime, many journalists still live in fear. Elías Cabral, a correspondent for the newspaper Ultima Hora and the TV station Telefuturo in Curuguaty, asked for police protection in February 2014 after receiving a threat over a story he had done on alleged embezzlement of public works funds at the local level. Cabral got police protection after Medina was murdered. "We do not trust the justice system or the security forces. We feel defenceless," he said.

Medina was protected by police officers from 2010 to 2013 due to threats, said ABC Color. Police discontinued the service in September of that year because it stopped giving protection to people in the absence of a judicial order, said their chief, Francisco Alvarenga, after the killing.

Thirteen years before Medina's death, his brother Salvador, also a reporter, met a similar fate and was shot dead for his radio reports on illegal activities in Curuguaty. Milcíades Maylin – one of four suspects – was convicted of his murder and sentenced to 25 years, although nobody was prosecuted for ordering the hit. Medina did not feel silenced by his brother's murder. But after his own death, other reporters might.

Medina's death has been a wake-up call for Paraguay on the allegations of links between some politicians and drug traffickers. However, Cándido Figueredo – who remains working in his "prison-like" home-cum-office – laments that the public outrage is fading, while the killers are still at large. He says he won't quit his job, despite the recent murders and the threats he has received. "I know my life is in danger and that traffickers may end it," he told Index on Censorship, "but this is what I know how to do and I feel I must continue doing it. If not, my conscience would bother me." ⌧

© César Muñoz Acebes
www.indexoncensorship.org

César Muñoz Acebes is a former Paraguay bureau chief for Agencia EFE newswire. He is now a senior researcher for Human Rights Watch

||||||||||||||||||||||||||||||||||||||||||||||||||||

Black hole for reporting

....

Mexican journalists and bloggers know the dangers to free speech that come from drug cartels and corruption, writes **Duncan Tucker**

Ever since the Mexican government declared war on the nation's drug cartels in late 2006, the country has consistently been ranked among the world's most dangerous places for journalists.

According to government statistics, 102 journalists were murdered in Mexico from 2000 until April 2014. At least another eight professional journalists have reportedly been murdered and two more have gone missing since then, bringing the total number of reporters that were killed or disappeared last year to at least 14.

Although drug cartels are believed to be behind most murders, the lines between organised crime and corrupt officials are often blurred. Freedom-of-expression NGO Article 19 noted last year that public officials were allegedly responsible for 60 per cent of the 330 documented acts of aggression against journalists and media outlets in Mexico in 2013.

Some parts of the country have become black holes for reporting, and many Mexicans now rely on anonymous bloggers for local security news. But this also brings great personal risk. In late 2014, the administrator of Valor por Tamaulipas (Bravery for Tamaulipas), a Facebook page with more than 500,000 followers that provides security updates in a northern state, announced his retirement. In October, their colleague María del Rosario Fuentes Rubio was murdered. Her killers published images of her blood-splattered corpse on her Twitter account as a warning to others. Valor por Tamaulipas' administrator initially stepped back from the project out of fear, but has since resumed work.

Valor por Tamaulipas has continued under new management and many other sites keep on bravely publishing, but there's little protection from authorities, who are either unwilling or incapable of guaranteeing their safety. ⌧

© Duncan Tucker
www.indexoncensorship.org

Duncan Tucker is a freelance journalist based in Guadalajara, Mexico

Lies and statistics

44(1): 80/83 | DOI: 10.1177/0306422015569439

Information on abortion and domestic abuse is being covered up in Nicaragua. **Nina Lakhani** reports from Managua on the restrictions on women's rights under President Daniel Ortega, and visits the organisation that's become a thorn in his side

IN A TINY, windowless office, tucked away on a leafy residential street in the Nicaraguan capital of Managua, four computer-savvy human rights activists spend their days scouring news websites and local police reports for the latest cases of violence against women and girls.

Magaly Quintana, founder of Catholics for Free Choice – an organisation that monitors violence and analyses data – meticulously follows up new cases while decoding official statistics on rape, femicide and abortion.

This modest outfit has become the go-to place for reliable information amid a deluge of policies by the Sandinista National Liberation Front (FSLN) government curtailing women's rights and suppressing related data. It has become a thorn in the ostensibly left-wing government's side by publishing easy-to-read bulletins that often contradict official reports.

Quintana's latest challenge is monitoring the consequences of the contentious new family committees, a new-fangled name for party political cells that have existed since the FSLN came to power in the revolution of 1979.

By order of a presidential decree, domestic violence victims must first seek counselling from these neighbourhood family committees, which are authorised to assess the seriousness of each allegation. The committees, which include party loyalists and church representatives but no trained experts, were introduced at the end of 2014. "This is the latest attempt to hide the reality of many women's lives in this country by making violence a family problem," said Quintana. "How many women will die waiting for these committees to decide their fate?"

Catholics for Free Choice was founded soon after Daniel Ortega, the former Sandinista guerrilla leader, won the 2006 presidential election and immediately began restricting women's rights and access to information. Ortega won the election, after three failed attempts, on a "Christianity, socialism and solidarity" platform. He won after striking what many believe was a cynical deal with the Catholic church to secure its support.

Within weeks, Ortega introduced a law criminalising abortion in all circumstances, without any prior public consultation. Nicaragua became one of five countries in the world with a total ban on abortion, even in cases of rape, or when the foetus is unviable, or when the mother's life is a risk. An unconstitutionality case filed to the supreme court in January 2007 by human rights organisations remains unheard. Ortega has described abortion as an imperialist policy.

Photo credit: Oswaldo Rivas/Reuters

ABOVE: Protesters in Managua demonstrate against the high rate of violence against women in Nicaragua

The pre-election deal also gave the church power to restrict sex education in schools. The existing guidebook, developed in conjunction with civil society groups, was withdrawn and replaced with a version that strictly adheres to church teachings on contraception and reproduction. The rhythm method is in; LGBT relationships and sex for enjoyment are out. Violent attacks against LGBT young people are on the rise, according to the children's rights NGO Plan International, which works with youth groups across the country. At least five people were murdered and six seriously assaulted in homophobic attacks in 2012.

The impact of the abortion law has been almost impossible to assess independently as the ministry of health has not published comprehensive obstetrics data since 2006. It

The pre-election deal also gave the church power to restrict sex education in schools

has, however, reported annual reductions in maternal deaths, which has won it international awards.

But in February 2014, the respected digital news website Confidencial leaked →

→ internal reports which suggest that official numbers were manipulated to hide maternal deaths that may have been preventable if the pregnancy had been aborted. The ministry of health reported 71 maternal deaths in 2013 and 51 in 2012. The leaked documents revealed the actual numbers were 87 and 71.

Faced with serious allegations the government adopted its now familiar response: silence. "The government plays with the numbers, with the truth, so what gets published often has nothing to do with reality. If they get caught, they say nothing," argued Quintana.

The abortion ban was introduced despite Nicaragua having one of the world's highest rates of sexual violence against girls. In

Official numbers were manipulated to hide maternal deaths that may have been preventable

2013, forensic doctors examined 6,609 sexual violence victims – of whom 51 per cent were under 13, according to the Institute of Legal Medicine. In 2012, 1,609 girls aged between 10 and 14 became mothers, according to the ministry of health.

Sex with a girl under the age of 14 constitutes statutory rape under Nicaraguan penal code. Catholics for Free Choice started analysing sexual violence figures published by the national police, the Institute of Legal Medicine and the ministry of health – which were often contradictory – to decipher how many perpetrators were being prosecuted. The police and ministry of health have not published figures since 2012. "They never say why it stops, it just stops," said Quintana.

There is deep-seated animosity between Ortega and the fiercely independent women's movement. It is widely believed that Ortega

has never forgiven the feminist leaders, many of whom fought alongside him in the civil war, for supporting his step-daughter Zoilamérica Ortega Murillo, now 46, who has accused him of sexually abusing her between the ages of 11 and 21.

"We believe that no one, not even the Daniel Ortega, should have immunity against such violence, and for that, women have paid a high price," said Juanita Jimenez, a veteran human rights lawyer with Autonomous Women's Movement.

Ortega Murillo eventually withdrew her case from the Inter American Court of Human Rights, but has publicly repeated the abuse allegations. Ortega and Rosario Murillo, her mother, have always denied the allegations.

Ortega remains popular, partly because the opposition parties are so weak, but every election since 2006 has been mired by allegations of fraud. The family's expanding business empire includes TV stations and newspapers.

"Power is increasingly concentrated in the hands of the Ortega dynasty, and its government is increasingly intolerant of any criticisms," said Gonzalo Carrion, director of the National Human Rights Commission.

The unlikely relationship between the church and Ortega continues, though not without incident. Just before the 2012 municipal elections, the Catholic Conference of Bishops publicly condemned election fraud and corruption, and said that Nicaragua "urgently needed to redesign its political system".

"Out of the blue newspapers and women's organisations got calls from the government saying the supreme court was finally going to hear the unconstitutionality abortion case," said Mayte Ochoa from Ipas, a global reproductive rights organisation.

"It was reported by the press, so of course the church stopped talking about transparency and fraud, and the appeal never went anywhere. It was all about sending a message to the church: we give you women's rights, in exchange you keep us in power."

There have been glimmers of hope. In 2012, amid growing pressure from the international community, Ortega's government passed the landmark Law 779 which outlawed all gender-based discrimination and obliged the state to support women and children leaving violent relationships. It also established specialist police stations, courts and prosecutors for gender violence offences.

But it immediately faced widespread opposition from church leaders, magistrates and lawyers' associations and ordinary men, who took to the streets to denounce Law 779 as anti-men and anti-family. Bishop Abelardo Mata said in a TV interview: "The new number of the beast is not 666, but 779."

The new family committees are part of subsequent reforms which have fundamentally changed Law 779. The government says the reforms promote family values, but for others they represent a dangerous backward step.

"The essence and objectives of Law 779 have been completely lost. It is now more difficult and dangerous for victims to speak out and get justice, at a time when growing numbers of dismembered and decapitated bodies indicate hate crimes against women are increasing. This machismo policy has put women's rights back 50 years," said Jimenez. ⊠

© Nina Lakhani
www.indexoncensorship.org

Nina Lakhani is a freelance journalist based in Mexico and regularly reporting from across Central America. She tweets @ninalakhani

IN FOCUS

long view

44(1): 85/102 | DOI: 10.1177/0306422015574214

When the Charlie Hebdo killings happened just a few weeks ago, the world's attention swivelled not just on to Paris, but also on the way terror and accusations of offence have been used to stifle debate. These are not debates only being had in France, so Index asked writers around the world to write short essays exploring those themes and how governments and writers have responded to them over the years

Laughter lines

44(1): 86/88 | DOI: 10.1177/0306422015574214

Co-writer of hit comedy television series Father Ted, **Arthur Mathews** takes a view on censorship and outrage in Ireland

MY FIRST "JOB" in London when I arrived there in the early 1990s was as a cartoonist for the New Musical Express (NME). Graham Linehan [his co-writer on TV series Father Ted] and I had come up with an idea for a strip called Doctor Crawshaft's World of Pop where pop stars at the time would be portrayed and presented in the style of George Cruikshank and James Gillray cartoons. I sent an example to Stuart Maconie (who was at the NME at the time), and he liked the idea. For about a year I sent a drawing a week into the magazine, "gently mocking" the antics and foibles of pop stars of the time: Sinead O'Connor, Carter The Unstoppable Sex Machine, Prefab Sprout – and some of the more established rock aristocracy like the Rolling Stones and Queen. The NME received only one letter of complaint – from Mark E Smith of The Fall. I think even Mark E Smith at his angriest wouldn't have gone any further than writing an irate letter, so I was never overly concerned about my personal safety. I don't ever remembering censoring myself, and didn't make any distinction between satirising artists I liked (Morrissey) or disliked (Duran Duran). The idea was to amuse the reader, not antagonise the object of the cartoon. I also reckoned that even if a rock star had managed to see the drawing and been mildly put out, he or she would soon be submerging themselves in an avalanche of alcohol, sex and drugs, and any mild offence taken would be quickly forgotten. Basically, I had neither the inclination to offend, nor the abrasive personality to deal with any adverse confrontation.

A few years later, Graham and I wrote "the clerical sitcom", Father Ted. Again, our aim was firstly to amuse ourselves (as well as potential viewers), and the idea of three priests living on a remote island appealed to us. Coming from rural Ireland, and feeling immersed in Catholicism – my father, especially, was deeply religious, and two of my uncles were priests – it was an area I knew a lot about. Father Ted was always more surreal than satirical (more Monty Python than Rory Bremner) and, despite its intended silliness, had many of the traditional aspects of sitcom at its core. In recent years I see it as more satirical than it appeared at the time. The dichotomy of three flawed, imperfect buffoons being the "link" between ordinary people and an all-powerful, eternal, perfect (although ill-defined and unknowable) supernatural creator of the universe was at the heart of the show. The idea that these three misfits were God's representatives on Earth was part of the humour. In Father Ted, the central characters may have been fools, but priests in the real world I grew up in were also flawed (as all human beings are), and to my mind, didn't seem particularly spiritual or unworldly; seeming to be as interested in horse racing or enjoying a small glass of sherry as to spreading the divine word of God.

The programme was first aired 20 years ago on the UK's Channel 4. At the time Ireland was still a very religious country. A "pro-life" amendment to the constitution had been passed as recently as 1983 in order to please the vociferous anti-abortion lobby. Divorce was still prohibited. (It was finally introduced in 1996 after a previous referendum in 1986 had been soundly defeated.) Even today, most of the schools and churches are controlled by the Catholic church, abortion remains illegal and a blasphemy law is still in place. Some 84 per cent call themselves Catholics – although, apparently, 62 per cent reject key parts of Catholicism such as transubstantiation. (I'm always intrigued by people who regard themselves as believers, but don't actually believe in the fundamentals of their faith. This doesn't apply to fundamentalists – obviously.) Modern liberal religious folk seem to have no problem in disregarding disagreeable portions of otherwise sacred texts when it suits them. It's similar to perusing a copy of the Rules Of The Road and saying: "Okay, I'll stop at red lights, but I'll travel at 150 miles per hour up a one-way street." (Obvious fertile area for satire there.)

Ireland has progressed, but I feel it's, at heart, a conservative country still coming to terms with the modern world. Needless to say, a recent suggestion that the famine of the 1840s could be a possible basis for a sitcom made by Channel 4 caused outrage. This was when the proposal was still very much at the "ideas" stage, but even the idea of it caused offence among the usual conservative reactionary elements.

Against this background, I wasn't surprised that many people were offended by Father Ted. And, coming from a Catholic family myself (like almost everybody else in the country), I understood that. I reckon that my older, conservative, rather fearsome priest uncle – who had died in 1989 and did not live to see the show – would have been gravely offended. However, because it was not an overtly satirical show, and most of the characters were actually quite loveable, it came, in time, to be seen as mostly harmless. Many (mostly younger) priests would laugh it off. One said to me once: "Sure you don't know the half of it!" Serious damage to the church would come a short time later with the revelations of sex abuse by the clergy and the scandalous regimes they ran in various Catholic institutions. The most that could be said about Father Ted was that it undermined

Under pressure from the church, the gloriously named Committee on Evil Literature was set up in the early years of the Free State to censor dangerous books and newspapers

the church in a country where it had always been venerated, and was rarely exposed to criticism. The tradition of opposition to the church from the left which existed in France never emerged in Ireland. There was hardly "the left" in Ireland at all. Almost everybody involved in the Irish revolution from 1912 to 1923, no matter how violent, uncompromising or fanatical, was a pious, mass-going Catholic. The emergence of an independent Ireland reflected their beliefs. Under pressure from the church, the gloriously named Committee on Evil Literature was set up in the early years of the Free State to censor dangerous books and newspapers. (The News of The World was banned, for instance.) The censorship board lasted until 1967, but →

→ its legacy of intolerance lived on. (Probably the most deliberately satirical piece of work I've done is Well Remembered Days, a bogus memoir written from the perspective of a Gaelic-speaking, rabidly Republican, pious Catholic civil servant. Random extract: "The 1950s were a very exciting time in Ireland. Censorship remained strict, government, by whatever party, was deeply conservative, and the country remained a largely agricultural and rural-based society controlled by the church.")

However, by the 1990s, the opposition to Father Ted that Graham and I experienced was much milder than it would have been 10 or 20 years before. We were never in danger of physical harm. Would we have created the show if we thought we would endanger

and hypocrisies ridiculed, and people can come away from debates with their points made forcefully and passionately without having to worry about their personal safety. That seems like a desirable society to me. To see it come under such ferocious attack as it did so recently in France is a shock to the system. ☒

© Arthur Mathews
www.indexoncensorship.org

Modern liberal religious folk seem to have no problem in disregarding disagreeable portions of otherwise sacred texts when it suits them

ourselves in some way? I doubt it. We would have written a sitcom about Formula One racing drivers. Father Ted was a mild satire, a million miles away from the provocative cartoons of Charlie Hebdo. While we never set out to offend anyone, we took it for granted that there would be no question of the show being censored, let alone taken off air, if people did take umbrage. Naturally I don't believe that all writing has to be political, polemical, or about challenging institutions and religion, but of course all writers should be free to do that if they so wish. We are lucky enough to live in a society which is tolerant, inclusive, and – this is important – with an ability to laugh at itself. It is also a place with few taboos – where everything can be discussed, its absurdities

Arthur Mathews has written for television since the early 1990s. He is best known for Father Ted (co-written with Graham Linehan) and Toast of London (with Matt Berry). He has also written for The Fast Show and Brass Eye. As a cartoonist he contributed to Doctor Crawshaft's World of Pop to the NME and The Chairman to the Observer Sport Monthly

Je suis José Carrasco

44(1): 89/91 | DOI: 10.1177/0306422015574214

For **Ariel Dorfman**, the Charlie Hebdo attack brought back flashbacks to writers' murders under Pinochet in Chile

SEEN FROM THE perspective of Latin America, the assault on Charlie Hebdo is both terrifying and familiar.

Not long ago, right here, in Santiago de Chile, not far from the house where my wife Angélica and I live part of the year, journalists and writers who dared to criticise the regime of General Augusto Pinochet, were systematically murdered – most of them tortured before being killed. Among so many, I remember above all José ("Pepone") Carrasco – first my student at the University of Chile, then my friend and fellow exile, finally a colleague who worked, back in Chile, at the semi-clandestine magazine, Análisis, which often ran satirical articles similar to the ones gracing Charlie Hebdo. The secret police came for José just before dawn on 8 September 1986 – and told him not to put on his shoes. He wouldn't be needing them where he was going. Some hours later, his bullet-ridden body was dumped on a Santiago street.

Terrifying, yes, and familiar. Just on the other side of the Andes, in nearby Argentina, hundreds of authors, intellectuals and reporters were arrested by the death squads and "disappeared", never to be seen again. Just to name one among the innumerable targets: on 5 March 1977, Rodolfo Walsh, one of his country's greatest writers, the pioneer of Latin American investigative journalism, awaited the arrival of the military at his home. Just the day before he had sent the Junta that misgoverned Argentina a defiant, insulting, mordant open letter, denouncing not only its human rights abuses but its

Over the last decade a slow massacre of journalists has been soiling, haunting, infecting Latin America, an almost invisible siege against press freedom

neo-liberal economic policies. His corpse has never been recovered. That open letter recalls the sort of passionate, sarcastic critique of power one could habitually find in the pages of Charlie Hebdo.

Both Chile and Argentina, of course, as well as other Latin American lands that suffered recent bouts of prolonged tyranny →

– Uruguay, Paraguay, Peru, Brazil, Bolivia, Haiti, El Salvador – are now democracies where media workers can, for the most part, do their job without fearing the knock on the door, the slit throat, the ditch at midnight.

And yet, over the last decade a slow massacre of journalists has been soiling, haunting, infecting Latin America, an almost invisible siege against press freedom. Not as dramatic or spectacular or on the fault-lines of Islam and the West as what happened with Charlie Hebdo, but nevertheless an assault that has been incessant and dreadful and methodical. Honduras, Guatemala and Mexico lead the way. Take the month of August 2013: three Guatemalan journalists were shot dead, including Luis de Jesús Lima, a prominent radio personality who dealt with all manner of controversial political issues. And Mexico: among dozens of reporters killed there, there's the case of Regina Martínez, who worked at Proceso, a hard-hitting weekly with which I habitually collaborate. A gang broke into her home,

Still, it ultimately matters that those who are not in danger let the world know – and especially those who would murder again tomorrow – that we will be not be silenced or let fear dictate what we are willing to express

and beat her viciously and then strangled her to death. She had been investigating ties between drug traffickers and local politicians in Veracruz. And Honduras: the most dangerous place for media workers in the world. On 9 March 2012, Alfredo Villatoro, a radio host was kidnapped in Tegucigalpa. Six days later his body appeared with a bullet in the head. He was dressed in military garb, with

an ominous red handkerchief covering his face. The death threats he had been receiving for many months had finally come true.

The world, basically, ignored these murders.

Truth be told, I tend to be ambivalent about the phrase currently used to identify with those persecuted: I am Salman Rushdie, je suis Charlie, todos somos Ayotzinapa [translated as "we are Ayozinapa" and being used to denounce the kidnapping of 43 Mexican students], even though I have often said those words myself or signed on to documents that exhibit such terminology. Clearly, there is something thrilling when millions of people across continents and oceans express their solidarity with victims of free expression. But I am also wary of this reaction. It is a bit facile and not completely genuine. We are not, all of us, Charlie. We were not, veritably, by their side when the gunmen came. And many of those who say those words, especially in the government and security forces, did not show yesterday the tolerance they proclaim today. Still, it ultimately matters that those who are not in danger let the world know – and especially those who would murder again tomorrow – that we will be not be silenced or let fear dictate what we are willing to express.

Maybe, after all, crying out "Je suis Charlie" is justified in this case because the attack on that journal was particularly savage and institutional and massive. It was meant to send a message not only to practitioners of the press, but also to a whole society. And thus it makes sense that all of society, in France and beyond its borders, voice as loudly as possible our grief and defiance.

And yet, seen from Santiago de Chile, seen from the vast perspective of a Latin America where the Honduran and Mexican and Guatemalan colleagues of Charlie Hebdo are dying right now, it is important to ask why the streets of our sad planet are not filled with hundreds of thousands of citizens declaring je suis Alfredo Villatoro, je suis

Regina Martínez, je suis Luis de Jesús Luna. Why did so few think to shout je suis Rodolfo Walsh? Or je suis José Carrasco?

Words like these probably will not deter future horrors. They seem inevitable in a world maddened with fanaticism and hate. But at least those who almost anonymously, in remote corners of the world, far from the Champs Elysées and the spotlight of the media, continue to speak out against stupidity and oppression will, one would hope, perhaps feel less lonely. ☒

© Ariel Dorfman
www.indexoncensorship.org

Ariel Dorfman is a Chilean-American writer. His latest book is Feeding on Dreams: Confessions of an Unrepentant Exile. He lives with his wife Angélica in Chile and in Durham, North Carolina, where he holds a distinguished chair in Latin American Literature at Duke University

Share access to the microphone

44(1): 91/93 | DOI: 10.1177/0306422015574214

Playwright **David Edgar** argues that pressure groups should push for more space on podiums rather than banning others from speaking

MANY POLITICAL MOVEMENTS start by calling for things to be banned. The British women's liberation movement began with a protest intended to stop the 1970 Miss World contest. In the late 1970s, I was involved in the Anti-Nazi League campaign to deny the National Front the right to speak to the nation on television through a party political broadcast. In 2004, Birmingham Sikhs picketed – and a small number physically attacked – a production of a play by a Sikh woman about sexual abuse in a gurdwara.

And, of course, 15 years earlier, Bradford Muslims burnt copies of Salman Rushdie's The Satanic Verses, and, in February 1989, the Ayatollah Khomeini issued his fatwa.

Later that year, demonstrations by hitherto silenced citizens across eastern Europe brought down six dictatorships, and demonstrated that – while not the only liberty – freedom of speech is a necessary precondition of all the others. Many young radicals, including Muslims, came later to that view. In 2007, former Muslim student activist →

→ Inayat Bunglawala, who had found the anti-Rushdie campaign emancipating and liberating, admitted that he had been wrong to call for the book to be banned.

It is, of course, this lesson which the Parisian killers refused to learn, understand or emulate when they attacked the French satirical magazine Charlie Hebdo. There are

Censorship by public pressure has increased hugely, turning the free speech argument from a debate about state power to one about consumer rights

many lessons to be drawn from the January events. It is possible to oppose Charlie Hebdo (or even call for it to be censored) and at the same time to protest wholeheartedly against mowing down its employees. But the main lesson is that, for those who believe in it, free speech is indivisible.

It is a particular irony, then, that some of the government leaders who marched through Paris in January immediately demonstrated a distinctly partial commitment to the principles of free speech. Within a week of the killings, the French police had arrested 54 people for "defending or glorifying terrorism". Such glorification has been a crime in Britain since Labour passed legislation that would – in theory – scoop up anyone lauding the Boston Tea Party, the Irgun or the ANC. Within days of the Paris killings, British Home Secretary Theresa May issued a code of practice that would authorise the police to access journalists' phone and email records. Last autumn, she announced plans to ban extremists from spreading, inciting or justifying hatred (and to prevent those who did so from accessing the airwaves).

Thus far, then, goes the commitment of the state to free speech. But the fight is com-

plicated by the change in the character of censorship. Since the 1960s, state censorship of the traditional kind – laws protecting a vulnerable populace from things they might like but would be bad for them – has been largely dismantled: the blasphemy law in England and Wales (though not Northern Ireland or Scotland) was finally repealed in 2008. At the same time censorship by public pressure or even intimidation from groups offended by various forms of speech has increased hugely, turning the free speech argument from a debate about state power to one about consumer rights.

In the United States, where the state was, and is, constrained by the first amendment, the power of groups to silence dissent was seen most clearly in the early 1950s, when an unholy alliance of the Catholic League of Decency and the American Legion (and many other bodies) seriously constrained filmmakers from making pictures that offended prevailing (or even unprevailing) norms on the portrayal of sexuality and the presentation of political opinion. Here in the UK, some newspapers that proudly stand against press censorship have in the past called for the proscription of plays, films and artworks that represent IRA leaders or certain types of criminal. (In 2004, the Daily Mail sacked a journalist who – in her spare time – had painted an image of Myra Hindley.)

Around the world, free speech campaigners are pitted not against the police but communities, from Hindus protesting at the depiction of their Gods in art, to US Christians mounting boycott campaigns against supposedly anti-family television shows. These communities include ones that feel themselves – and are – ignored, excluded and demonised. But the way to empower the silenced is not for them to silence others, but to spread access to the microphone.

The massacre of journalists at Charlie Hebdo is a bitter instance of the truth that it is the outsider and the dissident who suffers first when the principle of free speech is undermined. As Inayat Bungawala argued, on 27 June 2007 in a Guardian blog, that "the same laws that allowed Rushdie to have written the Satanic Verses are the ones that protect the right of Muslim authors ... to vocally oppose the government's calamitous participation in the invasion of Iraq". ☒

© David Edgar
www.indexoncensorship.org

David Edgar is a British playwright. His plays include Destiny, Albert Speer and Playing With Fire

Divisive language

44(1): 93/95 | DOI: 10.1177/0306422015574214

Best-selling Turkish novelist **Elif Shafak** says writers are keeping silent about their self-censorship

AFTER THE HORRIFIC attacks against the French satirical journal Charlie Hebdo and a Jewish supermarket in Paris, the world has turned into a Tower of Babel where there are too many languages spoken but too little, if any, real communication. Ever since those three days of terror in France, across the globe there has been more anger than sorrow, more emotional backlash than rational analysis, and more confusion than insight.

As heartwarming as it was to see millions of Parisians march against religious extremism and countless others show their solidarity via hashtags and messages on social media, we cannot ignore the fact that a rather disturbing cognitive gap is opening up between different parts of the world and different segments of humanity. Even in the face of atrocity, humankind is failing to speak the same language.

Among the political leaders who marched in Paris there were quite a few with a lamentable human rights curriculum vitae. While Saudi Arabia was quick to send a representative to France, the regime did not shy away from publicly lashing Raif Badawi, →

→ a liberal blogger, for his views. Israel, Russia and Egypt, among others, have been criticised for their double standards at home and abroad. Turkey, my motherland, has a shocking number of journalists and cartoonists either in prison or facing trial.

No doubt, the most moving response to the act of brutality came from cartoonists across the globe. With powerful images and few words they showed their unflinching support for freedom of expression. But those of us who cannot draw, and therefore must talk or write have done a poor job in general. With every aggrandising remark the cognitive gap widened.

Former French President Nicolas Sarkozy claimed: "This is a war declared on civilization." Soon after, the Turkish President Recep Tayyip Erdoğan announced: "French citizens carry out such a massacre, and Muslims pay a price." He then added: "Games are being played with the Islamic world, we need to be aware of this." Such statements only served to increase conspiracy theories, which abound throughout the Middle East. Meanwhile journalists, academics and writers lampooned each other.

The response to a book is another book. The response to an article is writing a counter-article. The response to cartoons is more cartoons, not fewer. Words need to be answered with words

So far, the language over Charlie Hebdo has been more divisive than unifying. Even the usage of conjunctions is a problem. After the tragedy, a top-level politician in Turkey tweeted that it was wrong to kill journalists, but they should not have mocked Islamic values. Never had the word "but" disturbed me so much.

The controversy had important echoes inside Turkey. The secularist newspaper Cumhuriyet wrote a powerful statement, saying that having lost some of their own writers to terrorism in the past, they understood so well the pain of the Charlie Hebdo killings. But the AKP government was of a different mind. The prime minister said printing the cartoons would be considered "heavy sedition" and they would not allow anyone to insult the Prophet. Accordingly, a court order was issued to prohibit access to Turkish websites that insisted in publishing Charlie Hebdo's recent cover.

In response, independent news website T24 openly defied the court ban and published the entire issue of the magazine. And people kept spreading the cover via their Twitter and Facebook accounts. It was interesting to see how many of these reactions came from people who were already tired of the AKP government's restrictive attitudes towards freedom of speech. As always, Turkey's social media operated as a political platform. Over the years as media freedoms shrunk visibly, the social media became more and more politicised.

Every journalist, every poet, every novelist in Turkey knows words carry a heavy weight, and they can get you in trouble. We know that only too well that because of a poem, an article, a novel, or even a tweet we can be sued, put on trial, demonised, even imprisoned. When we write, we write with this knowledge at the back of our minds. As a result there is a lot of silent self-censorship. Yet we find it rather difficult to talk about this subject, mostly because it is embarrassing.

As a Turkish writer both freedom of speech and freedom of imagination are precious to me. When I travel in Muslim-majority countries I often hear people saying "I am offended, don't I have a right to be?" Yet I believe we are making a grave mistake by focusing on the word "offence", and questioning whether art can be offensive or people have a right to be offended. We are stuck in a mental trap as long as we cannot manage to discuss violence and offence separately.

We need to divorce the two notions. It is perfectly human to be offended in the face of mockery, opprobrium or slander. That is understandable. Hindus, Jews, Muslims, Christians or agnostics, we can all feel offended by something someone says, writes or does. But that is where the line must be drawn. What is inhuman and unacceptable is to resort to violence and shed blood in response.

The response to a book is another book. The response to an article is writing a counter-article. The response to cartoons is more cartoons, not fewer. Words need to be answered with words. This simple equation is what we have failed to teach to both the younger generations and ourselves.

Let's be clear: this is not a clash of civilizations. It is not even a battle of religions. Yet it is a clash, and a deepening one, between two mindsets. The real chasm is between those of us who believe in pluralistic democracy, culture of co-existence and the value of diversity and cosmopolitanism, and those who have chosen to divide humanity into mutually exclusive camps: us versus them. It is a cognitive clash therefore.

As Sufis have been saying throughout the centuries, we are all profoundly interconnected. Globalism has way too often been interpreted as an economic and political phenomenon. Yet it also means that our futures, our stories and our destinies are interconnected. The unhappiness of someone living in Pakistan affects the happiness of someone living in Belgium or Australia. We must understand that in this complex web of relations any divisive rhetoric is bound to create more of the same.

Extremism somewhere breeds extremism elsewhere. Islamophobia spawns anti-Westernism and anti-Westernism spawns Islamophobia. A far-right racist in Germany might regard a Taliban man in Pakistan as his arch-enemy but in fact, they are kindred spirits. They share surprisingly similar narrow mindsets. And what's more, they need each other to exist and to thrive.

Let's be clear: this is not a clash of civilisations. It is not even a battle of religions. Yet it is a clash, and a deepening one, between two mindsets

We need to get out of the vicious circle of division and hatred before it engulfs us all. Together we must stand and speak up for pluralistic democracy and harmonious co-existence. At the same time, however, now is the time to think about the response we have given to the tragedy calmly and carefully. In this response lie the hidden important clues to our strengths and weaknesses as fellow human beings and the sharpest dilemmas that will continue to beset the world in the 21st century. ☒

© Elif Shafak
www.indexoncensorship.org

Elif Shafak is an award-winning Turkish novelist. She has published 13 books. Her latest novel The Architect's Apprentice (Penguin) was published in November

Blocked out

44(1): 96/97 | DOI: 10.1177/0306422015574214

While the rest of the world debates the finer points of free speech, China is still banning hashtags, email providers and even puns, says **Hannah Leung**

IN REACTION TO the terrorist attack in Paris, an editorial titled Press Freedom Has Its Limits was published by China's state-owned news agency, Xinhua. The writer argued that the Western press should "review the root causes of terrorism, as well as the implication of press freedom, to avoid more violence in the future".

The killings in Paris focused attention on journalism, freedom of speech, and pressure not to offend – issues familiar to anyone watching China in recent times. For years, China has not only censored news media,

No incident exposed the fears of the Chinese government more than the banning of puns in November

but actively blocked journalistic access. Well before the attacks on Charlie Hebdo, China was already extending its Great Firewall, blocking significant chunks of what it deemed unsuitable on the internet, in an attempt to restrict information reaching its citizens, information it believes would provoke public response and undo government policy. Some measures restrict journalist access to visas, or even detain journalists

themselves. (One recent victim is Zhang Miao, a Chinese woman working as an assistant to the German national newspaper Die Zeit. She has been detained indefinitely, following her coverage of the Occupy Central protests in Hong Kong.)

For foreigners accustomed to an open media, especially those who relish satirical political commentary, living in China has required serious workarounds. In 2009 when I moved to China, it was almost a given that expats arrived armed with a virtual private network (VPN) to access Twitter, Facebook and YouTube. Buried in all these platforms is also a great deal of ironic humour. Memes and other soundbites poke fun at current events and assumes a viewer is skeptical of political powers around them.

Photo-sharing app Instagram was not restricted until the end of September 2014, when the protests in Hong Kong were heating up. Photos of protesters uniting against the interference of the Beijing government were accompanied with trending hashtags like #UmbrellaRevolution, causing a swift blackout of the app on the mainland. During the Hong Kong protests, even pictures on WeChat, (China's rival service to free phone-messaging service WhatsApp) were censored. I imagine that in the eyes of the Chinese government, blocking such a visually rich social media platform would prevent its own citizens from rallying and supporting the other half of the "one country, two systems".

With such strict censorship in place, Chinese netizens rely heavily on coded languages, often substituting written characters with homophones: the written record may mean one thing, but if spoken, the message is quite clear.

No incident exposed the fears of the Chinese government more than the banning of puns in late November 2014, a real decree from the State Administration for Press, Publication, Radio, Film and Television. Print and broadcasters were urged to crack down on the "misuse of idioms", prompting witty headlines about the issue, including The Guardian's: "China bans wordplay in attempt at pun control". Already so deprived of many tools of their trade, journalists and netizens now find themselves subjected to arbitrary indictment in their use of language itself.

Even less of a laughing matter followed days before 2015 rang in, when Google's Gmail was blocked in China. Though connection to Google's search engine had been limited for years, the choice to block email access affected international businesses and personal interactions.

Now is the time to reflect on the balance between political commentary and the limits of free speech worldwide. But for those of us who work in and around China, it should also be a reminder that these conversations have less and less opportunity to even happen. And without unfettered email access to write "Je suis Charlie", how does one even start a conversation?

Take just one incident as an example. In July 2009, mass riots in Urumqi, the regional capital of Xinjiang Uighur Autonomous Region, left almost 200 people dead. Following the event, China dealt with the situation by shutting off internet access in the region for six months and limiting calls out of the area. More violence and unrest has erupted since; on 28 July 2014, over 100 people were killed in a premeditated terrorist attack on a police station in Xinjiang. But because foreign journalists who visit Xinjiang are either harassed or banned, it's hard not only to get transparency on what happened – let's say "review

China dealt with the situation by shutting off internet access in the region of six months and limiting calls out of the area

the root causes" – but almost impossible to even comprehend how to avoid further violence.

The issue the world has at hand is whether freedom of speech has its limits, whereas in China, it's whether such dialogue can even occur, on any platform. ☒

© Hannah Leung
www.indexoncensorship.org

Hannah Leung is a freelance Chinese-American journalist, based in Hong Kong

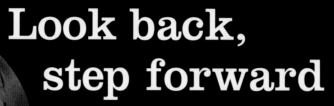

Look back, step forward

44(1): 98/100 | DOI: 10.1177/0306422015574214

Veteran journalist **Raymond Louw** examines censorship past and present in South Africa

SOUTH AFRICA'S MEDIA reacted with shocked revulsion to the news of the Charlie Hebdo massacre. Most journalists had never heard of the publication, but almost with one voice they condemned the wanton murders and the barbaric attack on freedom of expression, the core value of democracy, which they had often vigorously defended against government and other attempts to restrict press freedom.

They expressed their disgust and horror, on TV and radio and in print, at this unprecedented attack on the right of journalists and cartoonists to present unpalatable or even offensive views. Some, including this journalist, joined a silent protest by around 300 people outside the offices of the Alliance Française of Johannesburg, another protest of 100 people was held in Cape Town and flowers were laid outside the French Embassy in Pretoria.

Their anger was understandable given the history of censorship of journalists during apartheid, when the government passed more than 100 laws in attempts to prevent journalists from exposing the evils generated by the policy and the views of opponents.

Those journalists were also conscious of the attacks on media freedom by the new government and others in the two decades since the arrival of democracy. Among

these were recent legislative censorship attempts by the South African censorship board including the Protection of State Information Bill, the Protection of Personal Information Act, the Protection against Harassment Act, to quote a few. In the public sphere, there were the attacks by community protestors on journalists covering their violent demonstrations against government service failures – to prevent them from being identified – the SABC state broadcaster's ban on commentators critical of government and a failed attempt by the giant SA Breweries to persuade a high court to censor Laugh it Off Promotions for parodying one of its beer brands on a T-shirt.

After the Paris attacks, Nabeweya Malick, spokesperson for South Africa's Muslim Judicial Council, condemned the massacre. But he added: "There are limits to freedom of expression ... If someone criticises your place of work, your car, your shoes, these things are fine – but when someone insults, humiliates or degrades a personality that is connected to the heart of the Muslim, you have overstepped the bounds of freedom of speech."

Some journalists questioned whether the Charlie Hebdo cartoonists had ventured too far; whether a line should be drawn limiting the extent to which religious symbols could be satirised.

They also remembered the experience of Ferial Haffajee, when as editor of South Africa's national daily the Mail & Guardian in 2006 she published one of the controversial Danish cartoons of the Prophet Mohammed that prompted global protest. Haffajee, herself a Muslim, was threatened. A chain mail circulated with an instruction to kill her. Pressure was placed on her elderly mother. A Muslim organisation, Jamiatul Ulama, persuaded high court judge Mohamed Jajbhay (since deceased) to order the South African Sunday Times not to print the Danish cartoons. The judge wrote: "Although freedom of expression is fundamental in our democratic society, it is not a paramount value.

This freedom must be construed in the context of other values such as that of human dignity as the cartoon in question carried an 'insulting message' and sought to ridicule Islam and its founder." The Sunday Times decried it as a "serious blow to the freedom of the press".

Four years later, cartoonist Zapiro (Jonathan Shapiro) drew for the Mail & Guardian a cartoon of the Prophet Muhammad lying on a therapist's couch saying: "Other prophets have followers with a sense of humour." Jamiatul Ulama again tried to stop publication, claiming it could spark violence, but the court rejected its argument. However, the Mail & Guardian ombudsman, Franz Kruger, said publication might have been misguided, adding: "Why deliberately offend?" →

BELOW: Near the Charlie Hebdo offices in Paris, a copy of the magazine published after the attacks is put on a floral tribute as a memorial

→ Haffajee, now editor of weekly paper City Press, says that she would not print the Danish cartoon again. Yet, on 11 January she published 25 Charlie Hebdo front-page cartoons and in January printed a collage of cartoons from the "survivors' edition" with English translations. She explains that in sections of the ruling ANC she identifies a vein of deep intolerance and a threatening spirit which she equates to a national

ANC supporters, apoplectic at this desecration of Zuma's dignity, elevated the issue into a national crisis

consensus on the limits to free expression. The slaying of colleagues at Charlie Hebdo prevented her from supporting that consensus, she told the Daily Maverick's Rebecca Davis: "I'm going to go on the other side and become one of those free speech fundamentalists."

However, SA National Editors' Forum chairman Mpumelelo Mkhabela, editor of the Sowetan, was uncertain about the reaction of journalists. He told Davis: "I can't rule out the possibility of some [editors] taking a more cautious approach following the Paris barbaric attack – particularly, if the lives of staff might be at stake."

Even Zapiro, regarded as the country's most prominent and powerful cartoonist, is pessimistic. Davis quotes him: "I think it will have an immediate global impact and I'm afraid it seems inevitable that we will see the effects here. Put yourself in the shoes of a cartoonist doing a cartoon now, or a week or a month from now. Which South African cartoonist would not feel some apprehension right now? And the same goes for editors, columnists, authors, artists, musicians, publishers … The list is long."

On 15 January, he was proved right. The morning daily The Citizen apologised on the front page for publishing, on the previous day, the promotional handout of the upcoming "survivors' edition" – showing the Prophet Muhammad crying while holding a "I am Charlie" placard under the heading of "All is forgiven".

"The Citizen would never intentionally offend anyone's religious susceptibilities, especially in the manner used by Charlie Hebdo magazine … we deplore these killings, as we do any attempt to enforce censorship through violence. We uphold the right to free speech. Yesterday … we published an image which caused offence to many Muslim readers. We regret this oversight. We apologise to all who were offended," it declared.

That editor no doubt recalled the occasion when Haffajee's City Press angered ANC supporters when she placed on the paper's website a copy of a painting, called The Spear, by artist Brett Murray, showing President Jacob Zuma adopting a classic pose by Vladimir Lenin but with his genitals on display. ANC supporters, apoplectic at this desecration of Zuma's dignity, elevated the issue into a national crisis, burnt copies of City Press on Durban's streets and instigated a boycott of the paper.

But in issuing an apology The Citizen's editor highlights the sharp contrast in the attitudes of journalists on this issue, and especially of those who maintain the freedom of the press must be upheld at all costs to preserve democracy. X

© Raymond Louw
www.indexoncensorship.org

Raymond Louw is a former editor of the Rand Daily Mail and is chairman of the South Africa Chapter of the Media Institute of Southern Africa

Journalists are dying every day

44(1): 101/102 | DOI: 10.1177/0306422015574214

Murders of many reporters around the world go unnoticed, says **Richard Sambrook**

THE HORRIFIC MURDER of the Charlie Hebdo cartoonists in Paris in January produced a spontaneous reaction in defence of free expression from many around the world.

The fact that staff of a satirical magazine could be slaughtered for simply publishing comment and jokes seemed to cross a line that those adopting the "Je suis Charlie" slogan and gathering in protests believed essential to defend.

However, for many living beyond Western Europe or the United States, that's a line that has long ago and frequently been crossed. The brutal murder of journalists for nothing more than publishing their views is commonplace in many parts of the world.

Figures compiled by the International News Safety Institute show 105 journalists and media workers lost their lives in 2014, in countries including Syria, Iraq, Pakistan, Ukraine and Mexico, with shooting being the most common cause of death. According to INSI, an average of two journalists a week – every week – have lost their lives over the last decade. And in more than 90 per cent of cases, the killers are never found – often the murders are never properly investigated. Murder can be the most efficient means of censorship.

Some deaths, such as those of James Foley or Steven Sotloff in Syria, receive maximum media attention – and indeed are intended to intimidate and spread a bloody propaganda message.

Others are hardly noticed internationally. For example, Nerlita Ledesma who wrote for one of the Phillippines' biggest newspapers and was shot dead by a gunman on a motorcycle on her way to work in January.

In more than 90 per cent of cases, the killers are never found. Murder can be the most efficient means of censorship

Or Khalid Mohammed Al Washali, a correspondent with the Yemeni TV channel Al Masirah who died at the start of the year, one of four victims of a roadside bomb blast, allegedly carried out by Al Qaeda in the Arabian Peninsula (AQAP).

Or Robert Chamwami Shalubuto, a broadcast journalist for state media in the Democratic Republic of Congo, shot and killed by unidentified gunmen in December. →

→ Most of those murdered are not famous Western correspondents, but local journalists investigating crime or corruption – working on issues which embody the crucial ties between free expression and a healthy democracy. Because there is no doubt that the silencing of a critical voice damages free and open societies.

In the face of brutal intimidation, self-censorship becomes the new norm in some societies – allowing crime and corruption to flourish. The effective curbing of a free press

The growing bands of freelancers and bloggers, on whom international journalism increasingly depends, are more vunerable

can follow from the murder of even one or two key journalists, especially if they are famous and those who ordered their killings are not brought to justice.

Examples include the case of Novaya Gazeta journalist Anna Politkovskaya – killed in Moscow in 2006 – and the Sri Lankan Sunday Leader editor Lasantha Wickrematunge, who was shot dead in 2009 in Colombo after predicting his own death in an editorial published afterwards. Or the attempted murder of Pakistan TV host Hamid Mir who survived after being shot six times by unidentified gunmen in Karachi last year.

In many ways, those who work for established news organisations face fewer risks. They have employers with resources and support to offer and with influential voices. The growing bands of freelancers and bloggers, on whom international journalism increasingly depends, are more vulnerable – working on their own without support.

The United Nations has passed resolutions demanding member countries ensure the safe working of journalists – but resolutions have little effect with gangs in fractured countries. There has been much debate about including journalism safety in the UN's Sustainable Development Goals to be published later this year. Such a move would recognise the importance of free speech to a healthy society and would attract funding and support to ending impunity – the crucial first step in addressing this problem.

But there are also strong voices who do not believe the media should be included in the UN goals or that free expression is a "first-order" human right alongside the right to life and health. These voices must be countered.

It's essential that we all recognise that the killing of journalists is about more than just a right to speak. Free expression is crucial to the healthy functioning of any democracy, of any economy and to a society free of fear.

"Je suis Charlie" has to be about more than the victims of the Paris attack. It has to be about the murders of journalists taking place every week around the world. Because every time a journalist is killed for speaking out, or a murder goes unpunished, another corner of the world sinks into darkness. X

© Richard Sambrook
www.indexoncensorship.org

Richard Sambrook is professor of journalism at Cardiff University and chair of the International News Safety Institute

Screened shots

44(1): 103/106 | DOI: 10.1177/0306422015570538

As we approach the 70th anniversary of the end of World War II, Chinese cinema and TV drama are obsessed by the evils of Japanese invasion and occupation. **Jemimah Steinfeld** takes a look at pressures on the film industry to pump up the patriotic content

SHUAI'S NAME IS a homonym for "general" in Mandarin. His grandfather was a general in the army, his father a soldier, and Shuai too is in the military. Only Shuai's military does not exist in real life – it exists in a film studio. Shuai is part of an army of a different sort – one of thousands of actors who are conscripted into films and TV shows covering Chinese wars. And 2015 is their year. To mark the 70th anniversary of the end of World War II, China's state-owned film industry and television networks have received orders to increase the number of "patriotic" productions, of which wartime dramas are exhibit number one.

So why is Beijing encouraging these wartime movies with their anti-Japanese messages right now? Put simply nationalism has become the Communist Party's closest ally. Antipathy to Japan is used as a way to nurture patriotic fervour and detract attention from the home front. The genre goes in and out of fashion. Films about the war have circulated for decades, but it was during a legitimacy crisis two decades ago surrounding Tiananmen Square that the Communist Party first initiated an aggressive anti-Japanese propaganda campaign to bolster support for the government.

As for the recent push, 2015's China is not a secure place for the Communist Party.

It has found itself embroiled in a series of corruption scandals and faces a population disillusioned by many aspects of contemporary Chinese society. A common enemy can promote unity and provide a useful political distraction. One user of microblogging site Weibo hits the nail on the head: "Other than the [Japanese] 'devils', who are we going to fight? Corrupt officials?"

China has a long tradition of producing war movies, mostly drawn from the brutal conflict with Japan between 1937 and 1945, known by the regime as the Japan War of Aggression. During the Cultural Revolution, the movie Tunnel Warfare (1965) was seen by millions in China. The film depicts resourceful Chinese insurgents outwitting Japanese soldiers through the establishment of a network of tunnels.

Tunnel Warfare is part of a well-stocked library. According to Reuters, some 100 films and 69 TV programmes were produced in 2012 alone about Japan's war with China. After this bumper year, Xia Jun, a former China Central Television director, commented on the microblogging platform Weibo: "What's up with China's TV industry? Take a look around Hengdian [a major Chinese television studio] and you'll see 40-50 casts and crews fighting [Japanese] 'devils'." It is estimated that the genre occupies as much as →

ABOVE: An image from the film City Of Life And Death, (also known as Nanking! Nanking!) released in 2009

→ 70 per cent of the market, according to Reuters, and it's a share that will increase in 2015 if government orders are obeyed – and in China, these orders usually are.

For most of the 20th century, China's film and TV industry output was in the hands of the state, from inception through to completion. Under Chairman Mao (in power from 1949 to 1976), all movies had to serve a political purpose (The Party is great! Long live Chairman Mao!). Japan was lumped together with landlords, the former ruling Qing and other groups as "enemies" of the state, and these groups frequently appeared as the bad guys in films.

The state's control of the industry started to relax under the market reforms of Deng Xiaoping from the 1980s. Film studios became autonomous and today can make their own content. That's the theory at least. In practice they still have to get the approval of the Chinese censors if they want content to be aired domestically, either at the cinema or on TV. Having government approval is crucial. Government backing is even better – as shown in The Beginning of the Great Revival, a film about the founding of the Communist Party. When it opened in time for the party's 90th birthday in 2011, state-owned firms and schools were ordered to attend, and critical reviews were censored. Success was guaranteed.

By contrast, Jiang Wen's 2000 film Devils on the Doorstep was a flop. It tried to paint a more nuanced account of the war with Japan and was banned in China. The film, which won the Grand Prix at 2000 Cannes Film Festival, was accused of glorifying Japanese soldiers when it showed them exercising restraint towards Chinese villagers.

Mainland Chinese directors and producers are unwilling to spend time and money filming subjects the authorities might censor. It's less about government-produced propaganda and more about for-profit propaganda.

China Film Group (CFG) knows how to play the game. Along with a smaller firm in which it holds a 12 per cent stake, CFG controls over half of all domestic film distribution. The firm produces tales of love, disaster and, of course, martial arts. But the easy money is in the war. In recent years, CFG has produced Nanking! Nanking! (also known as City of Life and Death) about China's resistance against Japan, among other similar titles.

The genre has become synonymous with plots that rarely veer off a beaten track of good-versus-evil and acting that is derided as simultaneously wooden and over the top. Indeed, it has become something of a joke among Chinese viewers. Even Shuai, the Chinese actor quoted at the start of this article, is critical. "The plots are stupid and the characters I play are always the same," he said, adding that he feels under-challenged by such roles.

But there's more to the story. The Communist Party can use Japan as the prime enemy precisely because there are real grievances in China about the war. China's war with Japan was, after all, the longest conflict during World War II, with Japan invading China two years before Germany invaded Poland. It was also among the bloodiest. Some 14 million Chinese lost their lives during the eight years of conflict. Seventy years on, these movies might employ similar motifs and often in silly ways, but that does not mean the subject matter is a joke. For this reason there is demand for them beyond government offices. Older people in particular want to watch these shows and films: for them, the war against Japan is not ancient history.

"What is often missed in the Western press is how deep the feelings are among Chinese people about the issue. People can stoke it up but obviously there has to be a fire there to start with," Professor Chris Berry, a specialist in Chinese cinema, told Index. "It's hard to say one is a propaganda film and one is a commercial film. There are many different players involved and they all have different wants."

It is estimated that films about the war with Japan represents as much as 70 per cent of the market

Berry does believe these films are manipulated by the Chinese government for the purpose of propaganda, but he paints a more nuanced picture of what is going on behind the screens. He's also keen to stress that not all of the Chinese war films are terrible.

"Some of the films about Nanjing in particular try to provide a more complex picture. They try to depict Japanese soldiers who are not necessarily just grinning devils, at least in the world of feature films – TV series are more stereotypical."

Herein lies another problem with using the propaganda label too freely: Western commentators, in their haste to criticise China in this respect, are guilty of their own form of censorship. They effectively want to deny China the opportunity to talk about its wartime grievances. →

→ It's a point that Lu Yiyi, a journalist and expert on Chinese civil society, has noticed. In response to criticism of the 2011 Chinese film The Flowers of War, featuring Christian Bale, about the Japanese capture of Nanjing in 1937-38, Lu wrote in the Wall Street Journal:

"On the issue of China's dispute with Japan over the presentation of second world war history, there is a clear tendency for many Western media reports to employ double standards, underplay the sufferings of the Chinese people during Japanese occupation and turn the coverage of the history dispute into attacks on the Chinese government.

Western commentators, in their haste to criticise China in this respect, are guilty of their own form of censorship

"Numerous Holocaust movies have been made that portray Nazis as evil incarnate, but one does not see Western media describing them as anti-German propaganda that 'lacks subtlety'. Yet, when Chinese films on the Japanese occupation during second world war come out, western media reports are often quick to deplore their portrayal of Japanese soldiers as 'one-dimensional savages' and their 'demonisation of the Japanese army', despite acknowledging that the Japanese army had committed many atrocities, including during the Nanjing massacre."

"It's a mutual memory war," said Berry, citing the example of school textbooks in Japan as comparison, which primarily show the Japanese as victims of the atomic bomb. That is a pertinent point: both historically and today under Japanese premier Shinzo Abe, the country's war atrocities are downplayed and a heavy dose of lip-service is paid to Japan's powerful nationalist lobby.

The end of 2014 saw Japanese nationalists call for Unbroken, an American movie about a prisoner-of-war directed by Angelina Jolie, to be banned. Chinese film director Li Ying's 2007 tour de force Yasukuni was also banned by many Japanese cinemas. It examined the controversial war shrine in Tokyo from a number of different perspectives. In an interview with Index, Li, who currently lives in Japan, said that despite there being no official censorship body in Japan, certain topics are taboo. Criticising Japan's emperor during World War II is one such topic.

"There are a lot of anti-war films in Japan, but none of them directly face the Japanese emperor," he said. Undeterred by this past experience, Li has another film out this year, which again challenges popular convention about the war. Li wants to make people "rethink the tragedy of war" so that history is not repeated. At the same time he is acutely aware that he might receive unwanted animosity in Japan and admits that his producer is worried.

Viewers are right to be sceptical when watching "another China war movie". What it does show though is that controversies surrounding how the war is remembered transcend borders. Manipulation is not a one-way street. Some of the content that is airing in China this year is certainly propaganda; other content is part of a cathartic coming to terms with the past. It will largely be up to the viewer to decide which is which. ☒

© Jemimah Steinfeld
www.indexoncensorship.org

Jemimah Steinfeld is a contributing editor to Index on Censorship. Her book Little Emperors and Material Girls: Sex and Youth in Modern China (IB Tauris) is out now

Finland of the free

44(1): 107/111 | DOI: 10.1177/0306422015569711

Why does Finland always top press freedom lists? As it comes in at number one again in Reporters Sans Frontières' 2015 index, **Risto Uimonen**, chair of the country's Council for Mass Media, shares insight

THE FINNISH MEDIA knows it is in its interest to keep the government far away from the press. The consensus is that if the media does not keep its own house in order, someone else will come and do it for them.

In some countries, self-regulation is coming under increasingly heavy scrutiny, especially in the UK following the hacking scandal and the ensuing Leveson enquiry. Finland though provides the proof that it can work.

Finland's self-regulatory system, the Council for Mass Media in Finland (JSN), was formed in 1968 and since then it has been able to work without any serious interference from outside. Despite some inevitable criticism over the years, it has never lost the confidence of the press, public, politicians and influential lobbies.

The JSN was established by the Finnish Union of Journalists, the press and magazine industry, and the publicly funded Finnish broadcaster, YLE. It is successful because membership and compliance is voluntary, but it has no legal jurisdiction.

A press council is only credible if it can show the strength and willingness to set clear ethical boundaries. In Finland, we have been able to do this without using financial sanctions. If a media company is reprimanded, it must publish our whole verdict on its website and mention our resolution in the medium where the original mistake was made. The prominence of the correction must correspond to the seriousness of the original error. If there have been multiple factual errors in an article, or if the incorrect information caused significant damage, the editors must publish a new article in which the problem is identified and corrected.

These "shame punishments" work in Finland. Journalists and editors do not like to jeopardise their credibility in the public eye. They also work together to keep the system functioning, and there is a reason for this collaboration. Unlike many other countries, including Britain, Germany, Ireland and Sweden, Finland does not have a separate regulatory body for the press (including online content) and another for radio and television. We cover it all. This means one ethical code and one self-regulatory body. All publications and journalists are treated in the same way. Members find themselves bound by the same goal: to keep the media reliable, powerful and alive.

This is something that is taken seriously. About 95 per cent of the Finnish media works under the JSN's umbrella and all have committed themselves to our ethical code. The guidelines state that a journalist is primarily responsible to the readers, listeners and viewers, who have the right to know what is happening in society. The journalist must aim to provide truthful information and when the information is obtained, →

ABOVE: Risto Uimonen is the current chair of the Council for Mass Media in Finland (JSN), which was formed in 1968

Credit: Ida Pimenoff

→ it must be checked as thoroughly as possible, even when it has been published previously.

We find our members end up keeping an eye on each other. For example, in 2013, the JSN reprimanded a glossy magazine for not making a clear distinction between the journalistic content and commercial material. After the magazine, which belonged to the largest media corporation in Finland, protested publicly, a leading newspaper owned by the same company published an editorial politely contradicting the magazine and emphasising the importance of protecting self-regulation. Media companies and

journalists see our long-term objectives as more important than the short-term ill-feeling caused when a complaint is upheld.

The Finnish press is free to act as the watchdog of the mighty and criticise those in power. That is due to a very liberal press law and the fact that freedom of expression is protected by our constitution. Our press law gives the editor-in-chief of a news outlet the sole right to decide what to publish. This means, for instance, that the owners or chief executives of media companies, such as the Rupert Murdochs of this world, have no right to give orders to editors-in-chief about matters relating to content. If they are unhappy with the editor-in-chief's decision, they must fire him or her.

Our council gets roughly one complaint per day. The staff comprise two full-time and two part-time workers, and we work to a budget of less than $412,000 per year. We are regarded as being not only well functioning, but also efficient and relatively cheap. One way we keep costs down is by only paying a small fee to council members for their time. We do not cover the full cost of the losses they suffer when they take the day off to participate.

Our workload is also less heavy because there has never been an established tabloid press in Finland, only a couple of tabloidish magazines. They are also members of the JSN, and follow our code of ethics.

The council is formed of 14 members, each serving three-year terms. Eight members represent the industry and five represent the public. The chair, who gets the deciding vote, remains independent. Some people believe the public should be in the majority, but then our organisation would no longer be about self-regulation but about being dictated to by outsiders. This could endanger the whole system, as journalists would be less likely to co-operate.

Of course, we have had some difficult times. The previous chair of the council decided to quit suddenly in 2009, when he realised that he was going to lose a major case. The complaint dealt with a news item broadcast from the Finnish Broadcasting Company (YLE), claiming that the then prime minister of Finland Matti Vanhanen had taken a bribe of high quality timber for his house 14 years ago.

The complaint was not upheld by the council, which argued that the YLE had checked its source well enough. But the chair, Pekka Hyvärinen, wanted to condemn the YLE, because it had used only one anonymous source.

We changed our ethical code after that. Now the medium in question must clarify to the public how it has verified information from an anonymous source. The source, of course, must not be revealed. Recently, we have made additional changes to the code, including new, tough correction instructions and an addition to our media guidelines, defining how editors must handle user-generated material on their websites. Content that violates privacy and human dignity must

"Shame punishments" work in Finland; journalists do not like to jeopardise their credibility in the public eye

be deleted. It is a delicate matter because we cannot and do not want to give orders to the public and we do not want to limit their freedom of expression.

It is important for the JSN to be transparent and plausible, too. We must follow carefully what is going on in the rapidly changing media landscape and our system must be improve when needed. Otherwise the JSN and the whole system will quickly lose the confidence they have had for so long. ☒

© Risto Uimonen
www.indexoncensorship.org

Risto Uimonen is chair of Finland's Council for Mass Media

Media freedom in Europe

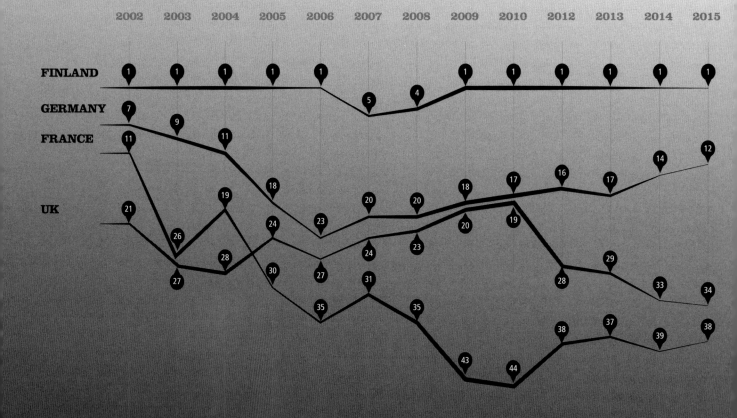

THIS CHART USES FIGURES FROM THE REPORTERS SANS FRONTIÈRES MEDIA FREEDOM INDEX, FROM 2002 TO 2015. FINLAND HAS CONSISTENTLY HELD THE TOP SPOT (ALBEIT SOMETIMES SHARED WITH OTHER COUNTRIES – MOST RECENTLY WITH NETHERLANDS AND DENMARK). AT THE OTHER END OF THE SCALE, BELARUS HAS THE WORST RANKING IN EUROPE.

RSF'S METHODOLOGY HAS CHANGED OVER THE YEARS AND MORE COUNTRIES HAVE BEEN ADDED, SO YEAR-TO-YEAR RANKINGS ARE NOT ALWAYS DIRECTLY COMPARABLE. YOU CAN EXPLORE ALL THE CHANGES AND THE NEW 2015 LIST ON RSF.ORG.

Opinion: Could the UK follow Finland's example?

Paul Connolly, *the Belfast Telegraph's readers' editor, discusses how he thinks the UK is trying to control its powerful and politicised media*

Can we have a press that is unruly, irreverent and cheerfully discourteous to those in power? Can we have one that is truly at arm's length from government? Yes. But all of this is meaningless if we do not have the trust of the public.

From my understanding of the Finnish model, trust is an incredibly useful, indeed powerful, weapon that helps to keep journalism on the right track and the politicians at bay. It is clear the Finnish public trust their journalists, and that is the fundamental transaction that validates the model.

But the Helsinki approach wouldn't be the correct model in the UK, for a number of reasons – many of them interconnected. Firstly, things have gone too far. Unfortunately, the debate on the future of the press became politicised and a cause célèbre of the left. Many on the left, though not all, saw it as a way to get to the press baron Rupert Murdoch, and the UK's Conservative Party.

Also, the press, or more correctly certain sections of it, handed its critics endless supplies of ammunition through phone-hacking, the practice of listening into people's voicemails and intercepting their phone calls; chequebook journalism and the debasement of popular papers through a corrupting version of showbiz journalism.

National newspapers were arrogant, treating corrections as a sign of weakness until the Leveson Inquiry, a judge-backed inquiry which was set up to look at the role of the police and newspapers in phone-hacking, changed all that. Before the inquiry, it was almost impossible for an ordinary person to get a correction into a national newspaper. Sometimes newspapers acted like thin-skinned bullies, unleashing bombardments on critics, rather than revelling in the cut and thrust of freedom of expression.

The UK's newly set up Independent Press Standards Organisation (Ipso), which seeks to regulate the press through a complex series of interlocking and commercially binding contracts, is such a system. Despite what the critics say, I do hope and believe it will finally disrupt the legacy of the, at times, too cosy relationship between the Press Complaints Commission and newspapers and will emerge as a pugnacious but fair regulator.

It will almost certainly never issue the theoretical £1 million maximum fine allowable under its rules, but provided it behaves in a way that says: "We'll do it if we have to", then the system will work for those who participate.

The obligation of those who have signed up, which is most of the UK press with some notable exceptions, is to operate a stringent and transparent process of recording, investigating and resolving, where possible, complaints. A system that will be subject to annual inspections.

Like most good ombudsmen, Ipso also contains protections for those it regulates: it can throw out groundless complaints and it also runs a whistleblower's hotline for journalists who believe they have been asked to perform an unethical action by a boss. Part of the Ipso contract states that journalists who legitimately use this hotline must not be subject to any disciplinary procedure. Although, as of February 2015, this hadn't been set up yet, provoking some criticism.

The Belfast Telegraph group has fully signed up to Ipso, and indeed the Northern Ireland media recently received its first intervention from Ipso on behalf of a person who was in the public eye and who did not want to be approached further by journalists. We were reminded that clause 4 (Harassment) of the Editors' Code of Practice prohibits harassment or persistent pursuit without an overriding public interest.

I hope Ipso will be a tough taskmaster. The industry needs it, and the public deserves it. Never again should the actions of a few London papers allow the stock of the great trade of journalism to sink so low.

© Paul Connolly
www.indexoncensorship.org

For more on the post-Leveson debate from Index, read: http://bit.ly/1edHGHg

Paul Connolly is the readers' editor of the Belfast Telegraph. He is member of the board of the UK Society of Editors

Is privacy more vital than national security?

OPINION: HEAD TO HEAD

44(1): 112/116 | DOI: 10.1177/0306422015571513

In the wake of the attacks in Paris, how far should governments go to get the balance between national security and personal privacy right? Member of the British House of Lords and internet guru **Martha Lane Fox** goes head to head with retired Major General **Tim Cross**

Martha Lane Fox

ABOVE: Martha Lane Fox

When it comes to balancing national security and personal privacy, I believe that your personal data should be your personal data, and that action should be taken based on a case that can be proven, as opposed to looking at everyone in society's movements and then targeting those who stand out. I am not a fan of the world we seem to be ending up in, and I don't necessarily believe that it is because of anything malicious. I think it would be better to have a system where your data is your personal property, and there then have to be the same restrictions applied as would be the case if someone wanted to enter your home and go through your belongings or intercept your post.

Tim Cross

Like fighting terrorism, governments have to "fight" with one hand tied behind their backs, but they cannot fight with both hands tied as some would clearly prefer. Individuals will understandably not want governments interfering with, or prying into, their personal privacy, but no one will thank any government if the banking system or consumer supply chains were to collapse. Monitoring cyberspace now forms a key part of any government responsibilities, and is (or should be) included in any national security strategy.

This said, if people fear the state is holding too much data on them unnecessarily and (rightly) demand some semblance of control over what happens with that data, then government is the least of their worries. Leaving aside the fact that government resources are scarce, the idea that some government

ABOVE: Tim Cross

employee is sitting in a room somewhere carefully sifting through everyone's email is fanciful. Intelligence and law enforcement have to meet certain criteria including necessity, proportionality and justification. This is absolutely the way it should be. But private firms have no such restrictions in place. Government intelligence and law enforcement agencies are rightly burdened by layers of legality, including authorisations, justifications and audit trails, but big corporations, particularly those whose primary public interface is through cyber means, use and exploit personal details for a wide variety of reasons. While these may sometimes include improving their services, more unpalatably they sell details on to third parties. This is absolutely endemic. Many companies will not allow customers to use their service unless they agree to terms and conditions that essentially mean losing control of their personal details and allowing them to be sold on to the highest bidders. The primary concern of business is making money. Not so with governments, whose intelligence and law enforcement agencies are about deterring/catching enemies and protecting the public.

Martha Lane Fox

It is impossible to say whether security is more important than privacy. I think it is largely dependent on circumstance. For example, in times of great national danger, and I would argue that this is not one of those times, there may be trade-offs that are acceptable to make us a community or country. However, ultimately it should not be a choice between security and privacy, or a case that you must choose one. It is, in fact, much more complex and nuanced than that and it depends wildly on circumstance, as well as the individual, timing, and all of the complexity you would expect to accompany that argument.

Tim Cross

The issue is what/whose "security" we are talking about. People's personal security, physical and electronic, is ultimately an individual responsibility, but even here governments have a role to play in trying to ensure that the correct regulations are in place, and policed, to give them the best chance of keeping/staying safe. Of course,

those states that repeatedly stress that security is undoubtedly more important than privacy such as North Korea, Russia, China and various areas of the Middle East get this wrong, but the wider security of community, society and/or a nation does rest with government. Indeed it is supposedly their first priority. Notwithstanding terrorist attacks like the most recent one in Paris, protecting critical national infrastructure against cyber attack, for example, is a key issue for any democratic government.

Martha Lane Fox

I don't think that the "new" digital age requires the implementation of a different set of rules surrounding privacy and security. The rules should stem from the ethics and morals on which society is based. I believe

It shouldn't be a choice between security and privacy, or a case that you must choose one

individuals should have a right to privacy. There is a very pernicious overtone to the argument that: "Oh, I'm not doing anything bad, therefore it doesn't matter if someone is watching me." Even if you are semi-conscious of being watched, there is a shift in the relationship between you as an individual and the state. The online world certainly has a greater complexity, and is clearly wildly different, but I do not think it means that we should approach it with an entirely different moral compass to how we would approach other areas.

Tim Cross

The principles probably remain much the same. It is the practical implementation of those principles that has changed, as it has done over the centuries with the →

→ arrival of new technologies. The problem today is that there is so much digital data/information around that monitoring it in an acceptable way is a very difficult trick to get right. There has always been a need for secrecy and a need for an ability to "encroach" on privacy, controlled by proper legal process, in order to protect the public.

We are constantly at war. Potential and real enemies are always collecting data and information

Exercising that is probably harder today then previously, but the right of personal privacy and freedom from unnecessary state intrusion remains vital. It is one of the lynchpins that separates us from repressive regimes and it must be protected and respected in all but exceptional circumstances. The actual wording of Article 8 (Right to Privacy) of the European Convention on Human Rights is pretty much spot on here.

Martha Lane Fox
I do think that perhaps different rules apply during times of war. We are very lucky that during the time of the internet's real growth we have not been in a brutal time of war here in the UK. I am sure you would feel quite differently if you were sitting in the middle of Syria right now, and I would argue that the terrorist threat does not class as a time of extreme war. It is very different to one country descending on another. And I really do find the use of certain language as an escalation of threat, quite unpleasant. So, although I think different rules apply here, I don't know what they are, and I am unsure as to when those triggers happen, but it is very important to challenge what the real threats are.

Tim Cross
In simple terms, yes, but the distinction between "peace" and "war" is not clear cut. In one very important sense we are constantly at war. Potential and real enemies are always collecting data and information. The reasons may be terrorist or criminal in intent, directed at both individuals and/or businesses, or they may be aiming at, for example, defence assets or critical infrastructure, such as energy/power supplies. These "enemies" have multiplied and become increasingly diverse, and they utilise cyber tools extensively whether working for a state, a group or alone on a political "cause" or just for anarchy and to gain kudos within the online community. Defence, particularly cyber defence, needs to be strong at all times because we are under *constant* assault.

Martha Lane Fox
I challenge the idea that the use of the internet was not originally predicted as a means of surveillance, and I do so partly because the invention of the internet came out of military investment in technology as a network for defence, a seed which was sown, arguably, at the time of Bletchley Park. So, I think it is slightly more nuanced than surveillance being simply overlooked. I think it wasn't thought of in the way we understand it now and that is partly because it would have been hard to imagine the proliferation of this technology being so rapid and the power it would have. For that reason I don't find it surprising that it has gone in directions we perhaps had not imagined.

Tim Cross
The internet was always seen as a surveillance tool by those few who really understood its potential. There is now a much broader understanding of the capabilities, for good and ill, but, the majority probably still do not understand its potential.

Martha Lane Fox

But I think some small percentage of people are aware of their digital security, and a huge majority are not, and I think some people care a great deal about it, and some people don't care at all, which might be due to a lack of information or even misinformation. What I do believe very strongly is that digital literacy, your ability to have a connection to the internet and to use the internet, is only one part of the greater picture of your life online. Part of it is having an awareness of what happens when you access the internet, about what information Facebook can save, or whether you understand that when you send a WhatsApp message it could be sitting on a server somewhere. We're not anywhere near being able to equip people of all ages with these skills, which are equally as important as the technical ability to use the web.

Tim Cross

The vast majority have no real understanding of what information they are placing into the "public" domain when they use the various commonly owned electronic/digital devices.

Martha Lane Fox

There are, of course, threats to security from hacking. You only need to look at what happened with the Sony hack recently to understand the scale of what is possible. It's naïve to imagine that this isn't a very real and present danger. When democratic governments are elected, some of their key responsibilities are to keep citizens safe and to protect their data, as well as government data. So hacking is a very profound threat, but you are much more likely to be run over by a car than to be involved in a terrorist attack. It is this sense of proportionality which often gets lost.

Tim Cross

Most hacking is relatively unimportant. It nonetheless disrupts individual and business life. Further, hackers are constantly attacking all firms/companies, hunting for private data. Some of these companies put virtually no investment whatsoever into their cyber security, endangering customers by leaving their information open for any savvy (or not so savvy) hacker to get hold of.

Martha Lane Fox

It has been well documented how Islamic State has been using the web, and just as other infrastructures can fuel potentially dangerous groups of people, for example the road networks or airline system, so does the internet. The only difference is that the transfer of information is much more rapid, much more difficult to track, and on a much more global scale. These dangers are not going to disappear, but I believe it is also very important, again, to keep them in proportion as there is a danger that the amplification of what happens online can create a massive amount of misinformation, and this perhaps goes back to the idea of educating people about the potential power of the web. I think there is a really interesting problem around how you teach anyone,

You only need to look at what happened with the Sony hack recently to understand the scale of what is possible

not just children, about authenticity. From my readings of the recruitment of terrorist networks, emerges this notion that people in disconnected places connect to people on the internet who feel authentic, who are running a terrorist cell on the other side of the world, and those people perhaps embark on a journey believing they are going to find something at the end of it that is more true to them than the community they are in, which could clearly be very →

→ wrong. It's about balancing what you find online with what happens in the "real" world and I think authenticity is going to become even more important.

Tim Cross

Terrorism is but a tactic. It has been around since Adam was a lad, but its ability to influence both individuals and governments is certainly greater today than before. As in dealing with all threats information is central. Data is collected from any number of sources, human and electronic, and that data is then analysed to produce information. The information is assessed to produce knowledge, which in turn allows decisions to be made. "Intelligence-led" operations almost always produce the best results and that applies to both terrorism and counter-terrorism. So constantly gathering data/information to assess and update potential risks and vulnerabilities is crucial. ☒

© Martha Lane Fox, Tim Cross
www.indexoncensorship.org

Major General (Rtd) **Tim Cross** (CBE) was commissioned into the British Army in 1971. He served in Northern Ireland, Macedonia, Albania and Kosovo. He was also the British deputy to the US-led Office of Reconstruction and Humanitarian Affairs, later re-titled the Coalition Provisional Authority. He is chair of the think-tank Theos

Martha Lane Fox is chair of Go On UK, a digital skills charity which helps people to get online. She co-founded travel website lastminute.com, and in 2013 became a cross-bench peer in the House of Lords

the **Leeds**

BIG BOOKEND

a rock festival for words

for the latest events & news visit

bigbookend.co.uk

f facebook.com/BigBookend
twitter.com/bigbookend

LOTTERY FUNDED | Supported using public funding by **ARTS COUNCIL ENGLAND**

ting ★ storytelling ★ workshops ★ theatre ★ books ★ poetry ★ readings ★ talks ★ music ★ perfomance ★ debate

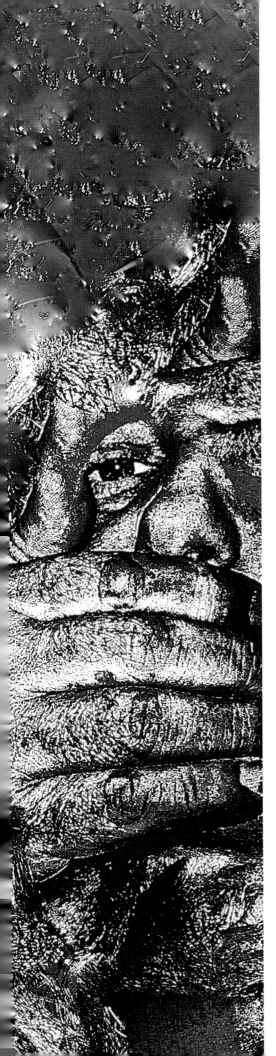

CULTURE

In this section

The state v the poets

44(1): 120/126 | DOI: 10.1177/0306422015569443

Kaya Genç interviews two Turkish poets – Ömer Erdem and Nilay Özer – about the struggles of writers in Turkey and introduces their poems, which are translated here into English for the first time

Ömer Erdem: "The state wants submission, and the poet rebels"

"Turkey has never treated her poets well," said Ömer Erdem, a Turkish poet known for his evocative verses. Well-read in both Ottoman and European modernist works, Erdem seems like a Turkish reincarnation of TS Eliot. "Since the Westernisation period began in the empire in 1840s, the state never stopped fighting her poets, irrespective of the party in power," he told Index.

Born in 1967, Erdem moved to Istanbul to study Turkish literature. After graduating, he started publishing poems in numerous Turkish journals and won the Cahit Zarifoğlu poetry prize in 2001. He was among the founders of the poetry journal Kaşgar. He published five poetry collections in the early 2000s and also wrote a weekly column for the prestigious book supplement Radikal Kitap. With his works getting printed by both left-wing and right-wing publishing houses, Erdem seems to have accomplished the difficult task of bridging Turkey's progressive and conservative cultural traditions.

Erdem describes writing poetry as the most political act in life. "A poet creates a language and a way of saying things, whatever the conditions of his society are like. After all, which fascist or religious regime has managed to completely silence the poet?

The great Turkish short story writer Sait Faik famously said that he would go crazy if he did not write." This is something Erdem also feels strongly, especially living in a country that does not stay true to its commitments to individual and artistic freedoms.

Erdem's attitude towards a poet's relationship with the state is simple. "The state wants submission, and the poet rebels against that. It is interesting to see how the Turkish state has not managed to produce a lasting international legacy or institution, while Turkish poetry has managed to preserve its uniqueness and originality." Erdem accepts that some Turkish poets have chosen to be servants of the state, redefining themselves as state artists and becoming guardians of its ideology in the process. "Who remembers their names, let alone their poems?" he asks.

Erdem sees the creation of a democratic tradition as vital for Turkey. "Democracy is necessary to lay out the legal foundations of brotherhood, to live with people who are different from us," he says. "For many years, people said that Turks and Kurds were brothers in this country. But brotherhood is not a legal term that makes living together freely and in equal terms a reality. Since the foundation of the republic, a top-down state structure imposed things on people. The state lacked self-confidence and was willing to use violence at the first opportunity."

ABOVE: Turkish police raided media outlets in December 2014 and detained 23 people nationwide. Here, editor-in-chief Ekrem Dumanli is cheered on by his colleagues as he is escorted from the headquarters of Zaman daily newspaper in Istanbul

Erdem is optimistic about the younger generation of Turkish citizens who are, he says, more eager to voice their demands. He characterises the political climate of the past two years as a chaotic wave of violence. He said: "When I look at what is happening to this country as a poet, I see missed chances and wounds that only get deeper."

Nilay Özer: "Artists can never stand with the state"

The protests in Gezi Park in 2013 pushed Turkey's arts scene to the point of no return, said Istanbul-born poet Nilay Özer.

"Defending artistic independence, freedom of expression and the right to protest became one and the same thing," she said. "A world of opportunities opened for poets who were

Independent authors and those who sided with the state have gone their separate ways

willing to give up on these." In other words, independent authors and those who sided with the state have gone their separate ways.

Özer, who belongs to the former group, said it was impossible for an artist to →

→ stand together with the state, or any political system. "Artists question every situation, and focus on human stories, rather than accept big generalisations." She is worried now to see fellow artists being subjected to intimidation and threats. "This undeniably tense new situation is a problem for anyone struggling to have greater freedom of expression."

When I look at what is happening to this country as a poet, I see missed chances and wounds that only get deeper

Özer, 38, spent her childhood in a working-class neighbourhood in the 1980s, a decade defined by the militarist ideology of General Kenan Evren and the Turkish Armed Forces. "My neighbours were mostly republican, secular people," she says. "Socialist ideas were prevalent among my student friends. There was also an understanding of Islam, which helped me see what morals meant for people." She wrote her first poem aged seven and, at 13, won the prestigious Milliyet newspaper's poetry prize.

Özer soon realised the publishing scene was totally controlled by men. She watched different groups compete for intellectual dominance and decided to keep her distance. "Intellectual groups turn into centres of power in time," she says. She also saw how the country's stark realities were quite different from those she grew up in. "Some people forced conservatism on to the country, and there was never-ending political turbulence, while Turkish and Kurdish youths got killed in the background. [...] I was living in a political and social era that provided wealthy material for my poetry," she said. "Poetry for me was not only an intellectual and aesthetic occupation, but also a shelter."

Özer – who was awarded the prestigious Cemal Süreya prize in 2004 – is fascinated by the wealth of the classic tradition, Arabic and Persian words and expressions, as well as Islamic, Indian and Persian myths. She is fascinated by modernist Turkish poetry, and also the influences of French, German, Russian and English literature. "As a poet I am not a traditionalist. I am someone who wants to feed on Turkish poetry's historical adventure and its rich poetic reserves." But she remains irritated that Turkish poets lack the facilities enjoyed by their European and US counterparts, and dreams of seeing more exchange programmes and artistic residencies in Turkey.

"Poetry offers a way to liberate your subconscious, and express the world," she says. In a country where the political atmosphere gets more suffocating with every passing day, she adds, poetry offers "a sense of vastness, lightness".

"It offers a sublime experience," she continued, "and gives us the chance to make the truth visible." ⊠

© Kaya Genç
www.indexoncensorship.org

Kaya Genç is a Turkish journalist and novelist, and a contributing editor to Index on Censorship magazine. He tweets @kayagenc

And then they shut her in a room

And then they shut her in a room
they even bolted it
they dangled a horse from a skyscraper
they crammed a sea into a picture
they wiped the eyes of a photograph from an
album

we've shut her up they said
we've shut her up in a room
they gathered in a park in the evening
they fired up their blood
they spoke here and there
they placed feed in the beaks of birds
and coffins on the backs of ants

she wrapped felt around her tongue
i'll punch myself to the ground like felt she said
then i'll sweat tiny tiny drops she said
steam of sweat she said flame of breath
poverty is no rope to my neck
it is a gourd violin she said

a pair of keys in the door
and a hairless wall were her close friends
her arms were longer than her legs
they shut her in a room
with no right
and no left
yesterday a shocked sun not informed of
winter
came to visit
and for three days she has been wiping
out the walls ...

ABOVE: Ömer Erdem

© Ömer Erdem
www.indexoncensorship.org

ABOVE: Nilay Özer

→ **Park**

take this pig now you walk it a while
the pig has no sin though it is ascribed
give it a wide leash everyone's neck deserves respect
and never ever look down on it
arrogance stings its pink flesh

the beggar on the corner doesn't like us
or the angst that separates the morning from the noontime
he doesn't like the nights walking askew
we leave a few words in his palm as we pass
everything will be okay … trust us …
what are words but an incitement of the tongue
and a fire that livens with pine cones and hazelnut shells

or reliving an evening viewed through a lover's earring
what else are words but the incitement of the non-existent
we passionately long for those beams
feeling for leaves deep upside-down
with a disembodied sexuality
that's why our shadows have become a dark bird
and we sit perched on the roots not the branches
we sat so that sitting would build up inside us
love is a short-range weapon we said
we learnt the alchemy of blending water and soil
because some of us needed glass eyes
because open wounds needed stitching
by that time our hands and feet seemed webbed
as if our fingers and toes formed in the park
we found a way to pluck the life-string from the candle

the houses reached the clouds take this death now and repeat
the sound of an accordion that has donated its organs
it can be heard on any street
we have hands that write underground and true
torture shames us all … save our bacon …
yesterday we passed on the pain of a conscious mind
no-one can ignore that even atoms of nothingness are being split
we discovered the sky's bell rings when we swing from the rain
we remember they want to erase it
how shameful for a flower to open so immodestly
they want to erase it we write it again
the ink of every age is blood
those gulping tea from etched glasses
don't know the grey taste of water flowing from hewn stone
that's why we have said we are a dark bird
on the mote into which our shadow fell
we sat so that sitting would build up inside us
music as a crossbow dance as chainmail
has the name of the rose changed now or a little later
who could count the woodlice poked with
pikes and javelins justice can't be counted
what remains of us
much more than us

there are no birds
but their shadows are on the rocks
following a commonplace war where the dead didn't return
the wind chimes meandering the branches
paper and ribbons wind roses
did we decorate the trees so that the wind would rustle more
or because we couldn't decorate the wind

→ *your son is gonna die in the next war ... habeas corpus ...*
we listen it seems everyone is speaking on a radio play
three women are tearing down a very old woman
bashing her about much too boorishly
hot water melts a frozen mind
what else are words but the incitement to life
and days in the creases of its skin
all religions divide ... fear builds walls ...
we were as intense and as timeless as the moment a match is struck
in fact the merchants were thin men
they knew the moment they looked whether our eyes would make ring stones
of course we were thrown into the fire we weren't salamanders either
poetry as a barbed harpoon
and to smile is better than all else we said
resist we said we branded its pink flesh
take this pig now you walk it a while ⊠

*The sentences in italics were taken from writing on pig-shaped balloons at Pink Floyd's The Wall concerts.

© Nilay Özer
www.indexoncensorship.org

Translations by John Angliss

Knife edge

44(1): 127/139 | DOI: 10.1177/0306422015569720

Lebanese playwright **Lucien Bourjeily** presents an exclusive English translation of his latest work, For Your Eyes Only, Sir. **Aimée Hamilton** talks to him about why his new play escaped the censors when his previous one didn't, and what inspired it

WRITER LUCIEN BOURJEILY believes that public pressure is the main reason his latest work, For Your Eyes Only, Sir, has not faced the same restrictions as its prequel.

His 2013 play Will It Pass or Not? was banned by Lebanon's censorship bureau, yet this new take, which includes scenes from the original, has been approved after some minor changes. It has already been performed in Beirut.

Bourjeily said this could be because of a change in personnel at the bureau, or more likely from the global attention, which came when the first play was banned. During his fight with the censors he was nominated for the 2014 Index Arts Award, and he also made international headlines when the authorities confiscated his passport last May.

Bourjeily's passport was taken when he tried to renew it before a trip to London's Lift festival. Initially he was told it could be six weeks before it was returned to him, but there was a sudden change. "People spread it all over the news. It went viral, everybody was talking about it, even internationally," he said. "They gave me back my passport and now they gave me permission to do the [new] play … it's a total reversal."

However, other cases of censorship in the country highlight that the bigger issues are far from resolved. Bourjeily mentions the case of Kareem Hawwa, who shared an article relating to the interior minister on Facebook, and was then arrested on allegations of slander and defamation. Bourjeily says: "The article isn't even written by this guy and then he got detained for four days and now he has a trial." It is unclear whether or not Hawwa also posted comments on the article, which may have provoked his arrest.

Bourjeily believes Hawwa was released on bail as a result of media exposure, and that the actions of the Lebanese authorities are greatly affected by how the outside world

Other cases of censorship highlight that the bigger issues are far from resolved

perceives them. "I think there's a schizophrenia with the Lebanese government," said Bourjeily. "They want to be the free government who accepts everybody, who doesn't oppress anybody, but at the same time they easily get offended. They easily get to abuse their powers. They don't accept criticism from activists and then they actually pursue them through the justice system."

Bourjeily says that in having For Your Eyes Only, Sir approved, activists have won a small tactical battle, but they have yet to win the war.

ABOVE: Scenes from a live performance of For Your Eyes Only, Sir at the American University in Beruit

→ **For Your Eyes Only, Sir**

In the censorship bureau of the general security directorate. Kareem (33), a director, is sitting on a chair.
Sergeant Da'ja enters the room. Kareem raises his hand.

SERGEANT DA'JA Why are you still here?

KAREEM The captain got a phone call. I'm waiting for him to finish, then I'll go in and see him again.

SERGEANT DA'JA Fine.

Jeanne D'Arc enters.

ABOVE: Bourjeily (right) plays Kareem/Writer in a live performance of For Your Eyes Only, Sir

JEANNE D'ARC Bonjour, I've come straight from the theatre. Do you recognise me? Jeanne D'Arc, the French-Lebanese actor. Perhaps you don't know me by that name... what about Umaima Alaywan?

SERGEANT DA'JA No, I don't recognise you.

JEANNE D'ARC From Chick Lit?

SERGEANT DA'JA No.

JEANNE D'ARC Waiting for a Brainwave?

SERGEANT DA'JA What are all these?

JEANNE D'ARC The Smoked Cat?

SERGEANT DA'JA The smoked *what?*!

JEANNE D'ARC They're just a few of the most recent dramatic works I've starred in.

SERGEANT DA'JA And what are you here for?

JEANNE D'ARC A month ago you gave me the all clear.

SERGEANT DA'JA What all clear?

JEANNE D'ARC The all clear... You know – the all clear.

SERGEANT DA'JA Do you mean a licence to perform?

JEANNE D'ARC A licence to perform, exactly. But today one of your men came and told me my play was an offence to public decency!

SERGEANT DA'JA Ah, okay, I'm with you now.

→ **JEANNE D'ARC** I've come to find out what's going on.

SERGEANT DA'JA Okay, okay, you can go in to see Captain Shadid and he'll explain.

They both enter the office of Captain Shadid.

SERGEANT DA'JA Sir, this is Mademoiselle Jeanne D'Arc.

CAPTAIN SHADID Please, come in.

JEANNE D'ARC Mr Captain, sir, I don't understand. Which part of my play precisely offends public decency?

CAPTAIN SHADID Mademoiselle Jeanne D'Arc, I haven't seen your play but I have been reliably informed that there's a scene where you take your clothes off on stage.

Who said that art had to be true to life? What is this play supposed to be – a documentary?

JEANNE D'ARC But I'm wearing flesh-coloured clothes. I'm not actually naked!

CAPTAIN SHADID Ah yes, but the problem is that under the stage lighting it looks like you have actually taken your clothes off ...

JEANNE D'ARC But I don't take my clothes off! Are you saying that if I wear a beige camisole in summer it's the same as being naked?

CAPTAIN SHADID That's not what I said. What you wear or don't wear in summer or at any other time of year – that would come under the remit of the vice squad. But the main thing is that this play is not fit for the stage.

JEANNE D'ARC Excuse me, sir. I'm Jeanne D'Arc. I'm celebrated worldwide for my support for the cause of Arab women. My aim is not merely to portray fallen women. I'll summarise the concept for you ... Basically, the play deals with a woman who is imprisoned by a man and the underwear represents the way he sees her – i.e. sexually – so at the end of the play she flings off her clothes to show that she is throwing off the concept of the masculine

ABOVE: Playwright Lucien Bourjeily

society, liberating herself from the idea that a woman is a sexual object.

CAPTAIN SHADID Absolutely, you're quite right. I don't doubt it for a minute, but as far as we're concerned this amounts to nudity.

JEANNE D'ARC Captain, sir, I'd be very happy to act out the scene and show you that it's not sexual, and you can see and judge for yourself.

CAPTAIN SHADID Here?

JEANNE D'ARC Yes, here. I have everything here with me. It will only take a couple of minutes of your time.

→ **CAPTAIN SHADID** Here? At the directorate? Well, it would be the first time we've had anything like this ... But, well, okay, please go ahead.

JEANNE D'ARC Thank you, captain ... But, sorry, would anyone from the office be able to come and help me? Because I'll need someone to act alongside me in this scene.

CAPTAIN SHADID Er, of course, no problem. Sergeant Da'ja will assist you. (*He calls Sergeant Da'ja in.*) Sergeant Da'ja, would you kindly join us for a moment?

Sergeant Da'ja enters the room.

CAPTAIN SHADID Sergeant Da'ja, I'll need you to assist Mademoiselle Jeanne d'Arc in performing a scene from her play.

SERGEANT DA'JA Me, captain?

CAPTAIN SHADID Yes, don't worry, it'll only take a moment.

Sergeant Da'ja is flustered. Jeanne D'Arc moves his shoulders, adjusting his posture.

JEANNE D'ARC I want you to just relax. Don't tense up. Relax your body and work with me. I want you to feel it.

SERGEANT DA'JA Er... sir, should I feel it?

CAPTAIN SHADID Hmm, yes, why not? Feel it a little.

Jeanne D'Arc puts on a bra and knickers over her clothes, and sits down with a darbuka drum. She taps out a fast rhythm, with a beat between each word of the following monologue.

JEANNE D'ARC You enslaved me, you locked me up... You robbed me of my soul... my destiny... my body...But no more! I've changed, I've set myself free!

Jeanne D'Arc stands up, pulls off her bra, launches herself at Sergeant Da'ja, grabs his suit and leans towards him with both passion and disdain.

Sergeant Da'ja leans back, moving with her. We sense that he melts in her hands more than expected.

CAPTAIN SHADID Straighten up, show some respect Da'ja!

Sergeant Da'ja straightens up and salutes.

SERGEANT DA'JA Yes sir, at your command.

JEANNE D'ARC But captain, if possible could he go with the flow for just a bit longer?

CAPTAIN SHADID But mademoiselle, we're ... Well, he is ... Well, okay, why not? Go with the flow a little bit longer, Sergeant Da'ja.

Jeanne D'Arc shrinks down, while Sergeant Da'ja looms over her.

JEANNE D'ARC My destiny ... my body ... But no more! I've changed, I've set myself free! I'm a free woman ... in a free society ...

Jeanne D'Arc pushes Sergeant Da'ja away from her, turning away dramatically.

CAPTAIN SHADID Lovely, lovely ... I mean you've quite reassured the directorate. (*He gives her a round of applause and Sergeant Da'ja does the same.*) To be quite honest there is a sexual element to it, but if I were feeling inclined to look sympathetically on your case, and if this is how you're dressed, well, then I wouldn't see a problem with it ... But you should wear clothes that aren't flesh-coloured, otherwise we won't be able to let the play continue.

JEANNE D'ARC But the whole point is that I've stripped myself of this sexual image ... that I've flung it off and gone back to nature ... the image of a woman's bare breasts ... it's an image of life and freedom ... a symbol of revolution, like the French revolution ... I want her body to return to nature ...

What I could do is I could come back tomorrow or even this afternoon and perform it for you in the proper costume, the flesh-coloured one? Then you can see for yourself, captain, that it's no different ... I assure you...

CAPTAIN SHADID Okay, fine ... Why not?

JEANNE D'ARC Oh, thank you, captain. I'm sorry for taking up your time.

Jeanne D'Arc leaves the captain's office.

JEANNE D'ARC Thank you Servant Da'ja.

SERGEANT DA'JA Sergeant.

→

→ **JEANNE D'ARC** Sergeant Da'ja, sorry. Anyway, you were great. Have you ever thought of taking up acting?

SERGEANT DA'JA Er, no.

JEANNE D'ARC You should really consider it.

Jeanne D'Arc leaves.

SERGEANT DA'JA You! Why are you still here?

KAREEM I'm waiting for Captain Shadid. He had a call.

Kareem says "freeze" and everyone freezes. He stands up and takes off the hat he was wearing.

WRITER Welcome! What you've just seen is an excerpt from Will It Pass or Not? – a play that was censored by the General Security Directorate's Censorship Bureau ... and I'm the playwright who wrote that play.

What you're going to see today is the play For Your Eyes Only, Sir – the sequel. It's about what happened to me and the producers when we submitted the script of Will It Pass or Not? to the censors.

Usually with films or plays, they make a sequel because the first one was a resounding success and the whole world saw it and loved it, and the producers want to cash in on its success with another film about the same thing ... Now I can't claim that Will It Pass or Not? – the first part – was a resounding success or that the whole world saw it, because in fact it was banned from the stage after just five performances. But it succeeded in one very important way: it proved that censorship is still alive and kicking in Lebanon and that the censor – God bless him – is still as vigilant as ever, tirelessly watching over the values and morals of the Lebanese people, because apparently our play threatened every one of them. So I'd like to take this opportunity to thank the censor, as he will be reading these words of this script, too, as of course this new play will also be subject to censorship before it makes it onto the stage.

So please close your eyes for a moment, dear audience, and imagine the civil servant in the General Security Directorate as he reads these words that I'm saying now, every word that I speak. Whatever comes out of my mouth is what he'll be reading. How do you think he'll feel when he realises that I'm a character in a play addressing him directly? (*He looks up*)

Hello sergeant! How are you? Or general or colonel or lieutenant colonel, or whatever…

- Yes, you … I'm talking to you.

That's strange – why am I looking up as though I were talking to God?

Anyway, keep your eyes closed. Now imagine the office with the chair that he sits on, the picture on the wall above his head, the files piled up around him, the pot of coffee, his mug, the suit he's wearing… Do you think he has a moustache? Grey hair? Anyway…

To whom it may concern, he who has censored us…

(*The writer points up at the sky.*)

We told you that the play was a satire and that it bore no relation to reality, but now it turns out that the actions of the censor have proven the opposite to be the case.

Yes, Mr Censor, we would like to take a moment to respond to you. Please take a deep breath before you finish reading. After all, we wouldn't want you to get confused between what is real and what is imaginary …

As you'll recall, Will It Pass or Not? was a play with five characters:

(*The characters enter the stage as the writer talks about them.*)

Sergeant Da'ja, Kareem the film director, Captain Shadid, Naha Shadid, a journalist and the captain's wife, and Jeanne D'Arc, who is also known as Umaima Alaywan.

In For Your Eyes Only, Sir there are also five characters, the counter-parts of those in the previous play:

(*The captain moves to the other side of the stage.*)

The colonel without a name.

(*Sergeant Da'ja moves to the other side of the stage.*)

The sergeant without a name.

(*Naha Shadid moves to the other side of the stage.*)

A journalist without a name.

$\rightarrow$

→ (*Kareem moves to the other side of the stage.*)

And I play the writer ...

(*The spotlight goes out on Jeanne D'Arc who is left on her own on the right hand side of the stage.*)

JEANNE D'ARC Wait a minute, what's my part in the sequel? Wasn't I the lead role in the first play? No one's said anything about my part being discontinued – I protest!

WRITER Your objection is quite justified, Jeanne D'Arc. I'm really sorry. I absolutely loved what you did in the last play, but what can I do? They banned us from performing it, because the play wasn't "realistic", and, well, I'm afraid there's nothing like you in real life.

JEANNE D'ARC Nothing? No *thing*? Excuse me, *Monsieur le Directeur*, I'm a renowned artiste and I won't accept anyone scrapping my part just like that. I want to speak to whoever is responsible. Who said that art had to be true to life? What is this play supposed to be – a documentary?

WRITER Please, you must tell him exactly what you've just said. We'll make sure he hears it.

JEANNE D'ARC What do you mean? Where is he? Where's he hiding? Is he here in this room?

WRITER No, no, he isn't here right now, or he might have stopped the play. But I assure you everything you say will be in the script and we'll submit it to the censor, to get his okay before we perform it. He can read it and if he doesn't agree with me, he can edit out your part or change your words.

JEANNE D'ARC What?! Are you trying to scare me? Are you saying there's someone who has the power to control me? And silence me if he wants to? Or make me say what he wants me to say? Who would even do that? What, are we in some kind of dictatorship? Who is this – Hitler? No, no, no! This is Lebanon, the land of freedom, of free women ... Well, I'll show you! I can say whatever I want! Ha! I'll prove it to you – I'll go and tell him right now!

Jeanne D'Arc moves her lips but we don't hear a sound.

WRITER Ah, you see, he's edited you out. So, I guess you won't be onstage undermining the esteemed officer's moral values, and meanwhile he is fulfilling his moral duty to the nation by curbing writers and creative people like yourself.

JEANNE D'ARC You're kidding – what is this?! *C'est impossible!* Okay, fine – what am I supposed to do? Tell him…

Jeanne D'Arc moves her lips but we don't hear a sound.
JEANNE D'ARC That's it – I've had it! I quit! I cannot continue with my art in such conditions! I don't know how you're still here. I'm going to take the lot of you to court!

(*She moves her lips but we don't hear a sound.*)

So let's emancipate ourselves from this censorship of art!

WRITER Wow. That is perhaps the most moving revolutionary manifesto I didn't hear! But never mind – the important thing is that he heard it before he deleted it … Don't worry, I'll find a part for you in For Your Eyes Only, Sir.

Jeanne D'Arc and all the other actors disappear.

(*On the left side of the stage*)

SERGEANT DA'JA So, what have you got?

WRITER A script for a play.

SERGEANT DA'JA Who's the playwright?

WRITER Me.

SERGEANT DA'JA And the producer?

WRITER March Ngo.

SERGEANT DA'JA Do you have all the necessary paperwork in place?

1   Letter and registered declaration of the organisation's intent
2   Municipality authorisation
3   Power of attorney on behalf of the director of said organisation
4   Identity card or passport and photo
5   Authenticated photocopies of all of the above

WRITER Okay, Okay.

The writer exits.   →

→ *Two days later.*

SERGEANT DA'JA Letter and registered declaration, municipality authorisation, power of attorney, identity card, all the necessary stamps, okay, and the script – yes. Where do you want to perform it?

JEANNE D'ARC *Bonjour*, I'm Jeanne D'Arc, You asked for me?

WRITER Jeanne D'Arc, what are you doing? Please, not now… I told you, I haven't got a part for you yet… I'm trying to think of something.

JEANNE D'ARC But God, this is so dull – you're both just going on and on … and nothing's happening. What's going on with this play? Where's the suspense? Are you the writer or what? Surely we don't have to teach you how to do it?

WRITER Okay, hold your horses, the suspense is coming… Can you please let me get on with it?

JEANNE D'ARC Okay, but just don't forget about me … I'm going to go and finish playing Candy Crush backstage.

Jeanne D'Arc exits.

SERGEANT DA'JA And where do you wish to perform?

WRITER Al-Madina theatre.

SERGEANT DA'JA When?

WRITER Mid-March.

SERGEANT DA'JA Okay. And what is the play about?

A moment's silence.

WRITER What's it about? It's a social satire.

SERGEANT DA'JA A social satire (*He's writing all this down*). And where is it set?

WRITER It's set in the censorship bureau of the General Security Directorate.

A moment's silence.

SERGEANT DA'JA Sorry – where?

WRITER The censorship bureau of the General Security Directorate.

SERGEANT DA'JA What do you mean?

WRITER It's set here – in an office like this. And there are characters like me and you.

A moment's silence.

SERGEANT DA'JA And what happens in this play? Give me a brief summary…

© Lucien Bourjeily
www.indexoncensorship.org

Translated by Ruth Ahmedzai Kemp

Lucien Bourjeily is a Lebanese playwright.
He tweets @lucienbourjeily

Index around the world

by **Aimée Hamilton**

INDEX NEWS

44(1): 140/142 | DOI: 10.1177/0306422015570804

SHOOTINGS IN PARIS threw a shadow over the first few weeks of the year, as journalists, cartoonists, police officers and members of the public were killed in a series of incidents, the first of which happened when gunmen stormed the offices of satirical magazine Charlie Hebdo. The resulting worldwide demonstrations, in remembrance of those who were killed as well as in defence of freedom of speech, drew enormous crowds together, with people holding pens in the air and #jesuischarlie placards. Index, alongside other freedom-of-expression organisations, joined with newspapers around the world to call for a co-ordinated publication of the magazine's cartoons to show solidarity.

Marking the enormous bravery of journalists and artists struggling against restrictions on freedom, the Index Freedom of Expression Awards will be held on Wednesday 18 March at London's Barbican Centre. The shortlist was announced at the end of January, whittled down from more than 400 nominees to just 17 across four categories – arts, digital, campaigning and journalism. There have been 68 champions since the launch of the awards in 2001; last year's winners were Egyptian rapper Mayam Mahmoud, Indian digital innovator Shu Choudhary, Pakistani journalist Shahzad Ahmad and Azerbaijani newspaper Azadliq. Other influential winners over the past 15 years include Russian journalist Anna Politkovskaya, who was murdered in 2006, and recipient of the 2014 Nobel Peace Prize Malala Yousafzai. Judging this year's awards, are: Martha Lane Fox, founder of lastminute.com and a member of the UK's House of Lords; Sir Keir Starmer, former UK director of public prosecutions; journalist Mariane Pearl; and Turkish author Elif Shafak. To see the shortlist, visit www. indexoncensorship.org.

Index recently appointed its second youth advisory board, made up of eight young people from as far afield as Iceland, India and Kuwait, who will hold their positions until May. The group comes together monthly to debate topical freedom-of-expression issues that are affecting their own countries and the rest of the world. Overcoming several time zones, the first meeting was held in December via Google Hangouts. Each meeting culminates in a question being chosen for the monthly Draw-The-Line discussion, which takes place online using the hashtag #IndexDrawTheLine. This year's first question was on how to balance religious freedom and religious extremism. The application process for the next board will begin in May 2015 for the June-to-November sitting; it is open to those aged 16 to 25.

Index's youth programme officer, Fiona Bradley, attended the British Youth Council Convention for the north-west in Wigan at the end of 2014. The council is made up of people from the region aged 14 to 18; youth workers and members of the UK Youth Parliament were also present. Index helped participants explore their understanding of censorship via a workshop that helped members identify how free expression relates to their daily lives. This is the third workshop Index has held with the British Youth

ABOVE: Index's Sean Gallagher attended the opening of Human Rights House Network's assembly in Ukraine, with (l-r) Arkadi Bush-chenko, chair of Human Rights House Kiev and the Ukrainian Helsinki Foundation; Serhiy Burov, chairperson of Educational Human Rights House Chernihiv; and Maria Dahle, executive director of Human Rights House Foundation

Council. The Draw-The-Line question was: are voting restrictions a violation of human rights? The group discussed and debated the possibility of the voting age being lowered to 16, which is one of the British Youth Council's current campaigns. Bradley also co-chaired a model UN day, where young people from the county of Buckinghamshire were appointed as delegates for the various nations, and came together to simulate a real meeting, discussing topics and strategies similar to those on the UN agenda.

In February, Index magazine launched its winter issue – with a special report on the Magna Carta: Drafting Freedom to Last – at the British Library. This year marks the 800th anniversary of the sealing of the charter by King John at Runnymede, and the launch coincided with the opening of an exhibition at the library, showcasing original Magna Carta manuscripts, as well as an original copy of the US Bill of Rights and the text of the Declaration of Independence, handwritten by former US President Thomas Jefferson. The exhibit will run until September.

Index CEO Jodie Ginsberg travelled to Canada in November to attend the Canada-UK Colloquium, an annual two-day →

→ conference that aims to promote dialogue between the two countries. This year's topic focused on the challenges within the online world and Index was the only civil society representative at the event. Index was arguing on the side of protection and promotion of civil liberties in the face of draconian legislation, which is restricting free speech online. UK delegates included Baroness Neville-Jones, MP James Arbuthnot and James Ball, The Guardian's special projects editor.

Ginsberg was also an expert witness at Google's advisory council on the "right to be forgotten" legislation, in Brussels in November. The new ruling, passed in May 2014 by the Court of Justice of the European Union, allows people to request search engines remove specific pages from search results relating to their name. She also attended BBC Radio 3's Free Thinking Festival at Sage Gateshead, where she spoke about big data and the cost of information.

Index's editor, online and news Sean Gallagher attended a series of events run by Human Rights House Network in Ukraine in late November, including the official opening of its Educational Human Rights House in Chernihiv and an international conference in Kiev. The conference covered various areas, in particular the human rights situation in Crimea and Eastern Ukraine; speakers included Valeriya Lutkovska, the Ukrainian parliament commissioner for human rights, and Boris Zakharov from the Ukrainian Helsinki Human Rights Union. The conference ended with a film on human-rights violations in Chechnya and a seminar commemorating the 20th anniversary of the start of the first Chechen war.

Index also co-produced a debate about artistic censorship with the Bush Theatre in London, as part of the Radar festival. The debate looked at various examples of theatre censorship, including the cancellation of Brett Bailey's Exhibit B by the Barbican in London. Panellists included Zita Holbourne, artist, activist and co-organiser of the Boycott the Human Zoo Campaign; Stella Odunlami, artist and cast member of Exhibit B; and Madani Younis, artistic director of the Bush Theatre.

Over the past three months Index also co-organised protests in London at the Azerbaijani embassy to bring to public notice how the government there is locking up democracy campaigners on trumped-up charges, and at the Saudi Arabian embassy to rally support for Raif Badawi, a blogger who has been sentenced to 1000 lashes for his writing. Badawi's case has attracted international condemnation. ☒

© Aimée Hamilton
www.indexoncensorship.org

Aimée Hamilton is editorial assistant at Index on Censorship, and is on the Index/Liverpool John Moores University post-graduation internship programme

Social disturbance

END NOTE

44(1): 143/145 | DOI: 10.1177/0306422015571882

News footage provided by readers and viewers has entered a new era, where we're faced with more propaganda, hoaxes and graphic detail than ever before. **Vicky Baker** looks at the increasingly tough verification process at the BBC's user-generated content department

THERE WAS SOMETHING rather sweet and innocent about the idea of user-generated content when it was first adopted by major news companies. It was about opening the doors to audiences, and making them feel valued. Those who sent in images or information from the scene were mostly trying to be helpful, enhance the understanding of a situation, or simply get their moment of fame.

Before long, this on-the-ground footage was leading the news bulletins and going viral within minutes. In the case of the Arab Spring, it was even instrumental in throwing over entrenched regimes. Then, alongside this increasing power, we started to see – particularly in the last year – the darker, more manipulative side of UGC. From Islamic State's (IS) propaganda to the information war between Russia and Ukraine, it had become an industry, not a byproduct.

"There are hoaxers now, trying to trip you up," says Chris Hamilton, social media editor for BBC News, which has faced increasing challenges in verifying content and deciding what to publish. "Some use it as a propaganda tool. And also, with the Sydney siege and Woolwich murder [of British soldier Lee Rigby by two Islamic extremists], we've seen events that are staged with online media coverage in mind." In both cases,

passersby or hostages were asked to film statements to post on the web.

The BBC's UGC department was first launched in July 2005 as a pilot project. One week later, the 7/7 bombings hit London and the new department leapt into action, collating witness accounts. The value was noted, the project went permanent, and the team now works 24/7, in the heart of the main, open-plan newsroom. On an average day, 3,000 pieces of user content are received – including images, comments, emails, SMS, and tweets. This swells to 10,000 during bad weather – the core British audience having a particular compulsion for sending in photos of their garden furniture in snow.

Much of this content is uncontroversial, but the images and videos sent from war zones or disaster scenes need particular attention. Verification involves looking at the core details – including when, where and how content was uploaded – and then assuming a quasi-detective role. Shadows can be a giveaway. So can accents. Is this old footage? Is it from another conflict? Has the soundtrack been dubbed to increase gunfire? Are those fighter jets on a major attack, or has one jet been mirrored to look like a squadron?

Alex Murray, a verification specialist within the BBC's team, remembers realising →

ABOVE: A mobile phone being used to capture pictures of an election rally in Tunisia

→ a small white square in the corner of a video from Libya was an expensive portable satellite, and thus it could not have come from by a casual bystander. High-end equip-

Expensive equipment can indicate a video has been funded by states, by rebels, even by NGOs

ment can indicate a video has been funded by states, by rebels, even by NGOs. "Videos are becoming increasingly professional," he

says. "In the early days, you'd be lucky if people remembered to turn their device around to shoot landscape. [Everyone instinctively shoots portrait, which doesn't fit a TV screen.] Now you have cameras that create broadcast quality."

We, the audience, hate to be duped, yet breaking stories are often embraced with a share-first, verify-later mentality. And if the footage fits in with the narrative we want to believe, we might never ask these questions. One of the biggest debunks of recent months was the "Syrian hero boy" video in November, where a young boy seems to risk his own life saving a girl from gunfire. A Norwegian filmmaker then admitted he'd staged it – in Malta – to "spur debate" about children in war zones. The BBC, sensing trickery, never posted it, but it had already been viewed millions of times. And, as Hamilton notes: "Many more people saw the hoax than the follow-up report, so many still believe it to be true."

The BBC may be doing its best to be responsible, but the platforms where users upload content directly have their own standards. The Sydney siege videos and IS beheadings were quickly censored by YouTube, but by that time they had already been copied and shared elsewhere. Less mainstream sites – such as LiveLeak – are quick to step in and publish the most gruesome videos. Justpaste.it, a Polish-owned site, inadvertently became jihadists' choice platform last year, because it allows users to post material without having to register and the simple design loads quickly on mobile phones, without needing a strong internet connection.

IS have also found a new trick in enhancing the credibility of their content: they are uploading their images to Archive.org, also known as the Wayback Machine, which is designed to be a internet time capsule. The not-profit organisation is aiming to collect a historic record of the web and won't delete footage. "It's a symbolic act," says Murray. "They are saying, 'We are doing this, so our

Timeline: how the BBC embraced user content

2004 The Asian tsunami in December saw footage filmed by tourists leading broadcasts.

2005 Major fire at Buncefield oil depot in Hertfordshire, UK, in December: viewers from a wide geographical area sent in photos and videos so the BBC could show the blaze's scale. The BBC launched its UGC department a week before the July bombings on London transport: journalists relied heavily on witness images and videos.

2007 User content, particulary from tourists, became crucial in covering an uprising in Burma, as journalists were not free to report.

2009 The Hudson River plane crash in New York in January was, says the BBC's Chris Hamilton, "when Twitter exploded into the consciousness of most newsrooms". Someone tweeted the first image of the plane from a rescue boat. "Previously he would have had to come home, connect his digital camera to his computer and then strike a deal with a newsgroup." In June, the Green Revolution in Iran saw mass protests against the officially declared election victory of Mahmoud Ahmadinejad. "Again, news organisations had limited access. We relied on content from liberal Iranians," says Hamilton.

2011 This was the watershed year. Hamilton explains: "There were the Norway attacks [by gunman Anders Breivik], the London riots, the Japanese tsunami and, the really big one, the Arab Spring. You saw the rise of hardware: smartphones were more prevalent and much higher quality. Events appeared on Twitter, Facebook and YouTube in realtime, and using these sites for news-gathering was no longer an esoteric pursuit."

2014 "We saw the rise of digital jihads," says Hamilton. UGC also played a huge role in covering the Gaza conflict from July to August, the US Ferguson protests in August, and the Sydney coffee shop siege in December. ⊠

content will be protected by the first amendment; it's part of a catalogue of our times'. People look on these sites for events of historic significance."

"Everyone that shares a video is in some way an activist," adds Murray. Whether they are hoping to help as a citizen reporter, or whether they have more sinister motivations. "They are partial; they are all sharing their experience from a personal standpoint."

Some people don't even realise they are becoming players in a much bigger story when they first hit upload. Take the bystander who posted footage of the final moments of Ahmed Merabet, the policeman, shot dead on the pavement outside Charlie Hebdo's offices in Paris. In a state of shock, the user made the split-second decision to post what he'd just seen on to Facebook. When he regretted it and took it down 15 minutes later, it was too late; it had gone worldwide. "I take a photo – a cat – and I put it on Facebook. It was the same stupid reflex," he told Associated Press.

But this is how news stories happen now: split-second decisions; a hunger for drama; a desire to share opinions and witness accounts instantly to be part of the action. But while audiences get more knee-jerk, those behind-the-scenes are getting increasingly savvy, from those producing the copycat propaganda to the small teams jumping through hoops to verify it. There are still viewers out there innocently sharing photos of their patio furniture in the snow, but the other side is fast-growing and powerful. More skepticism and patience would serve us well, but, in the hungry 24-hour news cycle, it's not something we are likely to see. ⊠

© Vicky Baker
www.indexoncensorship.org

Vicky Baker is deputy editor of Index on Censorship magazine

Download the Index App

A 30-day subscription gives you access to the most recent issue plus 3 years of archive content

Subscribe to the award-winning magazine on freedom of speech

Find out more:
email: subscriptions@sagepub.co.uk,
call: +44 (0)20 7342 8701, or
visit: indexoncensorship.org/subscribe